LIBERATING THE HUMAN SPIRIT IN THE WORKPLACE

LIBERATING THE HUMAN SPIRIT IN THE WORKPLACE

William Bickham

IRWIN
Professional Publishing®
Chicago • London • Singapore

This publication is designed to provide accurate and authoritative information in regard to the subject matter covered. It is sold with the understanding that neither the author or the publisher is engaged in rendering legal, accounting, or other professional service. If legal advice or other expert assistance is required, the services of a competent professional person should be sought.

From a Declaration of Principles jointly adopted by a Committee of the American Bar Association and a Committee of Publishers.

Irwin Professional Book Team

Publisher: *Wayne McGuirt*
Senior sponsoring editor: *Cynthia A. Zigmund*
Marketing manager: *Kelly Sheridan*
Project editor: *Christina Thornton-Villagomez*
Production supervisor: *Dina L. Treadaway*
Prepress buyer: *Jon Christopher*
Jacket designer: *Shot in the Dark Design*
Compositor: *ElectraGraphics, Inc.*
Typeface: *11/14 Palatino*
Printer: *Quebecor Book Group*

HD
57.7
B53
1996

Times Mirror
Higher Education Group

Library of Congress Cataloging-in-Publication Data

Bickham, William.
    Liberating the human spirit in the workplace / William Bickham.
        p.   cm.
    Includes index.
    ISBN 0-7863-0454-5
    1. Leadership.   2. Employee empowerment.   3. Organizational change.   I. Title.
    HD57.7.B52   1996
    658.3'14—dc20   95–44309

CONTENTS

PREFACE

Corporate practices of an earlier day are no longer appropriate. Yesterday's methods will not satisfy today's needs.

Earlier business organizations were a logical product of the needs of the day. Most were authoritarian in nature and effectively dealt with employees who were generally uneducated and who readily accepted orders from above. These organizations were typically hierarchical and militaristic in form and substance, with easily recognized levels of authority. As with the military model, these organizations were top-down in every important aspect, including decision making and communication.

SOME ORGANIZATIONS HAVE NOT CHANGED WITH THE TIMES

Unfortunately, there are organizations today that are still utilizing yesterday's approaches. They have failed to recognize the changes that have taken place in society and within the workplace. Today's workers are better educated. They are working for more than basic survival needs. As a group, they are seeking satisfaction and meaning in their work. When their needs are not met, some of these workers react in an openly aggressive and confrontational way. However, the majority react in more subtle ways, such as withholding their best efforts, which have a more profound and longer-lasting effect on both the individuals and the organization.

There is resentment and frustration among the workers in these outdated businesses. They have heard executives proclaim their belief in employee involvement and tell others about how much the company appreciates its workforce. However, nothing happens that would indicate anything but business as usual. Workers have been asked to make sacrifices during tough times, but there are no rewards when times improve. Secretly, they can share stories about the use of fear and intimidation that indicate very little change since their parents and grandparents suffered through the sweatshop tactics of an earlier and supposedly bygone time.

MODERN ORGANIZATIONS FOCUS ON THEIR PEOPLE

Some companies today recognize that the world has changed. The new relationships these organizations are building with their employees are based on cooperation rather than domination. They are fostering an atmosphere of involvement and commitment within the workforce. Responsibility is shared by moving decision making to the appropriate hierarchical level.

As a result, distrust and rivalries are being replaced by teamwork and unity of purpose. Workers recognize that they are an important part of the process, and much of the old "us" and "them" thinking is becoming a "we" approach to continuous improvement.

THE RESPONSIBILITIES OF LEADERSHIP

There is a saying that is attributed to Andrew Carnegie: "As I grow older, I pay less attention to what men say; I just watch what they do." This saying certainly can be applied to the practice of leadership. Leaders are not those who speak the most eloquently about the subject. Rather, they are the ones who do the things that cause others to recognize them as leaders.

Being placed "in charge" of other people is an awesome responsibility and one that should never be taken lightly. Such an assignment creates tremendous opportunities for the person in charge to create an environment that allows employees to do their best and to grow to new heights. Whether a person in a position of power views his or her role as *controlling* or *freeing* employees will determine what type of relationship exists between the two.

Those who are assigned a position of power over others are usually called *managers* or *supervisors*. It is in this context that I will be using these two terms. However, when I use the term *leader*, I will be referring to a person who is an integral part of the liberating process.

Throughout this book, I will be comparing the style differences between the *controlling boss* and the *freeing leader*. The chapters include vignettes that differentiate these styles through the words of those who are the most affected by a boss's approach—employees.

At the end of most of the chapters, there is a brief exercise intended to help the reader analyze his or her personal style. Included in each scoring section are some suggestions that would lead to a more *freeing* type of approach.

QUALITY—THE KEY TO BEING COMPETITIVE IN THE MARKETPLACE

Early in the first chapter of *Out of the Crises* (Cambridge: MIT Press, 1986), Dr. W. Edwards Deming states that, "Quality begins with the intent, which is fixed by management."

However, he also points out that improvement of quality requires total commitment by "everybody." In Chapter 2, he presents his 14 Points for Management, which outline the approaches he believes must be pursued if there is to be a "transformation of American industry."

With the 14 points, Dr. Deming calls for the development of a new relationship between management and the worker.

This book is about building those needed relationships in the workplace. It presents methods to increase the level of trust and interdependence throughout the organization. At the same time, it points out that both management and workers must assume responsibility for the continued growth and survival of the business that is providing for their basic economic needs.

Employee involvement alone will not assure a quality product or survival of the business. However, failure to recognize the employee as a partner in the quest for quality and innovation is a sure way to doom the company's efforts in the long run.

LOOKING AT LEADERSHIP

The material in this book deals with leadership and its applications in today's world. Its practical approach is based upon my 30-plus years in the trenches observing the actions of others and learning from their successes and failures as well as my own. It is written for those who are looking for practical tips they can apply in their own leadership efforts.

Part I, The Challenge: Dealing with Broken Spirits, deals with the types of past practices that have caused workers to lose heart and limit their commitment.

Part II, The Process: Changing the Operating Environment, looks at the elements of a supportive work atmosphere that encourage worker involvement.

Part III, The Approach: Employee-Centered Leadership, explores the type of work environment that fosters employee development and growth and that can lead to corporate community.

Part IV, The Commitment: To Accept the Responsibilities of Leadership, suggests ways that leaders can stay in touch with their surroundings and with the realities of their job performance, and it discusses the essence of the leader's job, while asking for a commitment to excellence from those who are willing to accept the challenge to lead.

The chapters that follow are a statement of my current philosophy of leadership. My beliefs and yours will continue to change as they are affected by new experiences. Therefore, any statement of beliefs is like a snapshot that freezes the action at a given moment. Hopefully, as you read this book, you will discover some ideas that will become a part of your next snapshot.

—*William Bickham*

ACKNOWLEDGMENTS

I wish to thank some special people who have made a significant difference in the ways that I think about business management and about dealing with others from a leadership position.

To my father, John R. Bickham, who is deceased. Besides the things that I learned growing up, I had the opportunity to work with him, in a manufacturing environment, for five years. Having worked during the depression, he was especially interested in recognizing the contribution of all workers and firmly believed in profit sharing. He made a difference in the lives of many workers.

To all those who have been or who are now responsible for *Industry Week* magazine. Thank you for the excellence that you bring to your readers month after month. There is no other publication that I read as faithfully as yours. I have been clipping and saving items of interest ever since Walter J. Campbell was editor-in-chief.

To Patrick Dolan, founder of W. P. Dolan and Associates. I had the opportunity to attend seminars given by Dr. Dolan in Lancaster, Ohio, in 1991 and 1992. His approach to business systems and his explanation of why changing an existing system is so difficult resulted in new insights that I have used continuously since that time.

To Max DePree. His book, *Leadership Is an Art* is the most important business book I have read in the last 20 years. Its impact on my way of thinking has been profound. If I could choose one person with whom I could discuss the subject of leadership, it would be Max DePree.

To Barbara Braham, speaker, author, consultant, and friend. Barbara has worked with my employer since 1987.

Her training skills are extraordinary, and her gifts are numerous. I have witnessed how others immediately relate to her due to the trustworthiness she exudes. Our many conversations about people in the workplace have been a major influence on how I approach the subject of leadership.

To John, David, Laura, and Steven, who are grown and out on their own but who will always be "my kids," and a major part of my being.

Finally, I would like to thank my wife, Susie, for 37 years of patience and understanding and for her unwavering support and love through the ups and downs of my business career.

I

THE CHALLENGE: DEALING WITH BROKEN SPIRITS

Employees are asked to commit themselves to making an organization a success. In return, they are too often subtly or overtly treated like serfs, subject to the will of a master.

Chapter 1

Paper Towel Mentalities

Recently, I was talking to Susan, an employee of a company that has been going through "rightsizing," the current buzzword for cutbacks in the workforce.

She related how surprised she had been to learn that an acquaintance named Jim was losing his job. Jim was a bright and energetic young man. He had worked long hours on several company projects, had made several suggestions that had been adopted within his department, and generally displayed a high level of enthusiasm and drive.

Susan recounted her final conversation with Jim as he prepared to leave. He was distraught as he told her what his boss had said to him. "He told me that while I had done several good things since joining the company, I had also 'ruffled a lot of feathers' and was viewed as a 'maverick' who wasn't a 'team player,'" Jim said. The boss's final words of advice were, "Wherever you end up, you should try to fit in better and quit trying to make a name for yourself. What companies want are employees who do good work within the system."

Susan said that Jim left in a somewhat bewildered state. Tears welled up in her eyes. "You know," she said, "I shouldn't be so surprised. My company has always had a 'paper towel mentality'; they just use people and then discard them without a thought."

Ralph is a production worker for a small company that produces parts for the automobile industry. One evening, he joined a group of parents at a local restaurant after a high school football game. After a while, the discussion turned to work-related topics. Ralph listened for a while and then added the following comments.

> You talk about hostile work environments! You ought to spend some time at our place. The superintendent's favorite quote is, "If you don't like the way we do things here, why don't you get a job someplace else?" We're always butting heads, and nobody trusts anybody. They say, "Don't think; just do what you're told." So that's what we do. Sometimes you know you're running scrap, but after you've been told that your opinion doesn't matter, you just keep your mouth shut and wait to see how long it takes the smart guys to figure it out.

The rumor around town is that Ralph's employer is in trouble and that layoffs or even a shutdown are on the horizon.

DISCOURAGING CHANGE

Stories like these abound. Workers are told that their brains are not needed on the job. They are given no respect and are stripped of their dignity. They are asked to "do it right the first time" and to produce work with "zero defects" but are told to keep their opinions to themselves. Often, they receive little or no training on the proper methods of performing the job.

Think back to your own initiation into the work world. Do you remember the answer you got the first time you asked why something was done a certain way? You were probably told that when you had been with the organization a little longer, you would understand how things were done. How about the first time you made a suggestion that something might be done a different way? Chances are that it was a long time before you took a chance on speaking out again.

DETERMINATION OF THE WORK ENVIRONMENT

Over the years, I have grown to believe that motivation comes from within each individual and that a person in a leadership role can only create a motivating environment to which others respond in varying degrees, according to their own makeup.

If this is true, then what happens when a person in a position of power misuses that power? Does he or she create a demotivating environment to which others also respond in varying degrees? I believe that the answer to this question is yes.

Regardless of how motivated an individual might be to do his or her best, an atmosphere of distrust, rumors, threats, and intimidation will eventually take its toll. If an individual is controlled and smothered in an environment that stifles learning, creativity, and freedom of expression, growth is either impaired or blocked until conditions change.

I worked at that place for nearly 15 years. I started right after high school. Funny thing was that I hated it almost from the very first day. The supervisors were all bastards. If you saw one coming, you knew something was wrong. They were always on your back about production quotas, and they never had a good word for anyone. Another thing was how filthy the place was. The lunchroom was cruddy, and the rest rooms should have been condemned. You really caught hell when some customer returned something because it was defective, but only a supervisor could stop a line because of a defect. If

QC found a problem, they had to go find a supervisor. Even they didn't have shutdown authority.

Well, things just kept getting worse. When we lost customers, people got laid off. Finally we were down to just one partial shift. Just when it looked like curtains, they sold the company.

The new owners came in, and the changes started the same day. First, there was a gigantic clean-up, fix-up, paint-up campaign. Everything, including the lunchroom and the rest rooms, were put in first-class shape.

Next, the assembly lines were redone, one-by-one. Not only did they give us the equipment we needed, but every few feet there was a red button that would stop the line. When we started having meetings with the supervisors that they had brought in from some of their other locations, they told us that any of us that spotted a defect were authorized to stop the line so it could be corrected on the spot.

It's been nearly three years since the company changed hands. We're back to full shifts, and business is in good shape.

I used to grumble and bad mouth the old company and, every now and then, I'd call in sick, just because I didn't want to go in that place. Now it's a different story. I've had two straight years of perfect attendance, and I've won a couple of awards for suggestions that I've made.

All of us are sure glad that someone came along that cared enough to save our jobs and also treat us like part of the answer, instead of like part of the problem.

(Factory worker)

THE DEVELOPMENT OF A "NO-CHANGE" APPROACH

How does an organization develop a "no-change" philosophy? What work experiences influence a firm's top executive? Usually, a CEO rises to the top position by working his way through levels of authority within that organization or one with similar characteristics. The very fact that he continued to advance is proof that he learned how to play the game. Chances are, this climb took a major portion of his work life and required tremendous personal sacrifices.

By the time such an individual assumes the top position, he is comfortable with the familiar trappings of the organization and knows which buttons to push to keep things humming along in the same old way.

As one might expect, the winner in such a long and difficult struggle is often a strong-willed, self-confident individual who appreciates what the organization has accomplished in the past. He is comfortable with perpetuating the operating characteristics that have led to his personal success. In building a staff to assist in this effort, it is normal for the executive to surround himself with people who see things in the same way. Realistically, why would he do otherwise?

This approach can, however, lead to an unexpected problem. Typically, a strong-willed person may be easily annoyed by the observations of others, especially if any observation is viewed as nonsupportive or contradictory. Therefore, if someone in the executive's advisory group should take exception to some idea or approach that the executive proposes or supports, this individual may be labeled a troublemaker, a maverick, or, even worse, disloyal. How this person is to be viewed by others within the organization will be communicated through the boss's direct and indirect reactions. The boss's reactions will also send a clear signal to everyone else as to whether they are to function as a true advisory group or merely as a support group for the status quo. If the message encourages conformity by a group that is already biased by past successes and that has worked too long and too hard making it to the top to commit "position suicide," then the wheels have been set in motion for the executive to receive little or no meaningful feedback.

Over time, the boss who operates in this type of atmosphere will lose touch with the realities of his own organization. His top staff will sometimes alter facts that are presented to him so they are more in keeping with the desired results than with the realities of the day.

If the people are rewarded for being agreeable and for reporting "good news" and punished for raising questions and for bearing "bad news," obviously the boss will receive the type of information he wants to hear and that he rewards. Future planning will then result in a continuation of past practices, since there is no reason to tinker with success. The problem is further compounded if the organization continues to make money in spite of itself. In these cases, even the slightest suggestion of change is usually greeted with a sneer and a comment something like, "Have you looked at the bottom line lately?"

THE EFFECT OF A CLOSED ENVIRONMENT

Some incidents have long-lasting effects on those on the receiving end. Careers have been altered by events that, at the time, seemed to be blown out of proportion.

Alan, a 53-year-old bank vice president, tells about a career-changing incident that happened almost a year ago. He was a member of the bank's executive committee, which was preparing to hold its annual planning session for the upcoming year.

In the opinion of most of the bank's employees, one of the bank's weakest links to its customers was its 15-year-old phone system. The system had no state-of-the-art features such as call waiting or voice mail. As a result, when employees were away from their desks, phones rang incessantly. Even worse, when an employee was busy with a customer, the phone rang on that employee's desk until someone else answered it and took a message or until the calling party gave up. Either way, a customer usually ended up dissatisfied.

Because of both employee and customer complaints, the phone system had been the subject of discussions several times previously. Usually, the bank's president would lament the cost of automated systems and comment on the loss of the "personal touch" that such systems create, and then the subject would be changed.

Lou, the bank's president, opened the planning session with a few welcoming remarks that included a call for participation and openness in order to make the day meaningful.

The group then began a SWOT analysis exercise in which the participants were asked to list the strengths, weaknesses, opportunities, and threats they believed were affecting the organization. Everything was proceeding smoothly until Alan mentioned the "antiquated phone system" as a company weakness.

Lou immediately exploded. "I'm getting damned sick and tired of hearing about our phone system! There is nothing wrong with our system that a better customer service attitude wouldn't take care of. We are not going to change our phone system. Did you get that Alan? I said we are not going to change our phone system! I should be able to expect support from this group instead of an atmosphere that smacks of undermining and contempt for my wishes! In case any of you have forgotten, I'm the one in charge! I'm the one who has to answer to the board, and I'm the one who will decide when it is time to talk about a new phone system!"

What followed was a period of deadly silence, a decision

to take a short break, and a changed atmosphere that resulted in an early end to the day's program.

In the days that followed, Lou told several key employees that Alan was responsible for ruining what had begun as a successful planning session.

In the months that followed, Alan was aware that he was slowly but steadily excluded from meetings and other events in which he had previously been a participant. Reasons were always given, such as the meeting had a subject that didn't directly involve him, but it became painfully clear that Alan was now an outsider. A couple of times he questioned his exclusion from a particular situation, but again he was always given polite but firm reasons why his presence wouldn't be required.

Alan is now waiting to see the attendance roster for this year's planning session. He has also begun a confidential job search.

Within his bank, Alan is viewed by many as a victim of Lou's unpredictable temper, unclear opinions, and vengeful attitude. At the same time, everyone is much more guarded in Lou's presence, lest they suffer the same type of wrath.

At the local chamber's recent small business luncheon, Lou gave a talk entitled "Customer Service is Priority Number One." He dwelt on the idea that employee involvement is a key to anticipating customer needs. He wowed the crowd. Some were heard to admiringly say what a great boss he must be to work for.

DEALING WITH A DEMOTIVATING ENVIRONMENT

In some cases, the situation remains static because the person in charge is really not a leader. The result is a long-term demotivating environment. When this is the case, some employees may leave in search of fulfilling environments. However, other employees will have personal circumstances that may make it impossible for them to leave. These employees will remain and learn to deal with their surroundings in one way or another.

For example, a blue-collar worker who is earning decent money and accumulating seniority that affects a benefits package would be hard-pressed to leave, especially if he has a family depending on him. In this type of situation, even the strongest person may become disillusioned and, with time, possibly resentful and bitter. Ralph, the production worker in the earlier example, was not proud to admit that he sometimes knowingly runs defective material. In fact, having observed him as a no-nonsense type of parent, who often tells his kids why he expects them to be responsible for their actions, I found his comments to be out of character.

Listen to the words of other workers as they talk about the places they are spending their work lives:

> I can be a little league coach, a board member of the Little League Association, and committee member at my church, but when I get to work, they tell me that they don't need my input.
>
> (Hospital technician)

> I just go to work every day and do what I'm told. A lot of the time, I think about what I've got planned after work. That helps make the time go faster.
>
> (Auto mechanic)

> Women aren't getting ahead here like they deserve, but that's hard to prove. Besides, I need my job, and I can't afford to be known as a troublemaker.
>
> (Bank teller)

> Do you remember those little figures of three monkeys that people used to have on their desks? One had its eyes covered, another had its ears covered, and the third had its mouth cov-

ered. The saying that went with it was 'See no evil; hear no evil; speak no evil.' It took me a long time to figure it out, but those monkeys ought to be our company logo. Under the monkeys, in gold letters, it could say, 'To get ahead in this company, see nothing; hear nothing; say nothing.'

(Department manager)

THERE MUST BE A BETTER WAY

It used to be fairly common to refer to workers as "hired hands." Some employers still act as though all they are interested in is a strong back or an able pair of hands. Employers who view workers as "things" are likely to exhibit a "paper towel mentality" towards employees.

We can better utilize the potential being wasted in situations like the ones discussed above. Work environments in which managers and supervisors rely on power and control must be replaced by those that emphasize growth and freedom.

Everyone wants to invest his or her time and effort in situations that matter. A business's ability to compete over the long term in today's global economy requires the best efforts of every employee on a sustained basis. The type of personal commitment needed from each employee cannot be ordered or demanded. It must be earned by a leadership group that leads by example, makes the effort to explain why employees should want to invest their time and effort, and cares enough to repair the broken spirits to which they, or their predecessors, have contributed.

Taking Stock

Instructions: For each statement, circle the number that most closely represents how often that statement is true for you. Use the following as a guide:

Almost never	Seldom	Occasionally	Frequently	Usually	Almost always
0	1	2	3	4	5

1. Do you get angry when employees ask "why" questions? 0 1 2 3 4 5
2. Do you interrupt employees who are trying to make suggestions? 0 1 2 3 4 5
3. Do you blow up at an employee who comes to you with organizational "bad news"? 0 1 2 3 4 5
4. Do you criticize an employee in front of others? 0 1 2 3 4 5
5. Are you hostile with others if you're having a bad day? 0 1 2 3 4 5

Scoring

Total your scores from the five questions.

If your total score is from 18 to 25: Your workers may avoid contact with you when possible. You need to reflect upon the negative impact that you are having on them and work to win them back.

If your total score is from 9 to 17: You are sending your employees "mixed signals." They may view you as someone who must be approached with caution. Work on being consistent and be more open in sharing your opinions with them.

If your total score is from 0 to 8: Your employees are probably comfortable around you and picture themselves as part of a team. Maintain your present work relationship and look for ways to help them grow.

Chapter 2

The Effect of Doubt on Working Relationships

When the participants in a work relationship doubt one another, every aspect of that relationship suffers. Decisions are second-guessed, and efficiencies are lost.

> My supervisor is a real gem. When any of us go on a break, we have to give her a slip that says what time we left our desk and what time we are due back. Then, afterwards, we have to go back in her office and let her know that we are on our way back to work. She always checks the time, and if she's not satisfied you get what we all call, 'the evil eye.' She just sits there and stares at you. Sometimes I feel like I'm back in grade school.
>
> (Clerical worker)

As a manager, you will usually get the type of performance you indicate that you expect. If your words and actions suggest you don't trust your workers, they will become less and less spontaneous as they take what they view as necessary precautions to protect themselves. You may interpret these defensive reactions as suspicious and an indication that you were right to question their ability to be trusted in the first place.

This type of negative downward spiral often leads to more and more doubt and is very difficult to stop because both parties are confident that the other is to blame.

> We were having a big storewide sale, and my supervisor told me that a department up on the sixth floor was short two people and she would appreciate it if I would go up there and

help out for the day. I went up and reported to the supervisor. She asked me to tag some blouses, then she picked up the phone and called someone. I heard her say, 'She's here; thanks for the help.' I asked her who she called, and she said it was my supervisor. She said, 'She wanted to know when you got here.' You know, our relationship has never been the same since. I always feel like she's watching me, and I don't think I have ever given her a reason to doubt me.

(Salesclerk)

The manager kept telling everyone that she had an open-door policy and that we could come to her with our problems. So, one day when my supervisor was off, I went up and told her about some of the problems we were having in our department and that our supervisor wouldn't listen. The next week, the manager showed up in our department. She took all of us, plus our supervisor, into the conference room and proceeded to repeat everything I had told her. She didn't mention names, but she may as well have. Our supervisor responded that none of the things were true. Everyone else was scared to speak up, so we ended up getting chewed out for not working together. So much for an open-door policy. It will be a cold day before I open my mouth again.

(Claims adjuster)

DOUBT HINDERS PARTICIPATION

You might assume that companies which operate in an atmosphere filled with suspicion and doubt will perform poorly. This is not necessarily true. Doubt operates more as a deterrent to an open and friendly atmosphere than as an unfailing indicator of financial failure. However, it is safe to assume that, whatever the level of a company's success, it would be even more prosperous if it did not have an undertone of doubt.

Doubt also limits involvement and free participation. Employees will hesitate to make their own decisions, even about routine tasks, preferring to avoid the possibility of having their intentions questioned. When asked for their opinions, they may become defensive, seeing such a situation as a possible setup.

We had just wrapped up the cleanup from one hell of a snow storm. Many of the people had worked long, hard hours, clearing the roads and then clearing them again. Conditions were really bad, and everyone pulled together to get the job done. The county engineer put out a memo thanking everybody for their effort, and, at the same time, he scheduled what he called a "debriefing session," so everybody could share their ideas on how we could do even better the next time.

The day of the meeting, we all assembled in the meeting room at starting time. There were coffee and doughnuts, and there were two easels set up in the front of the room. He started the meeting by thanking us all again and then asked us to just sound off with anything about the storm. He had two of our supervisors stationed at the easels, with markers in hand.

After a few minutes, one of the guys asked if we could get some other locations for meals, since we were limited to just two locations in the whole county, which caused some lost time, plus neither place had the greatest food. The boss kind of chuckled and said, 'Don't think we can do much about that. Those folks have always worked closely with us on meal amounts. They help us make sure that no one is doctoring any bills.'

There were some more questions, but every answer included some kind of suggestion that we had to be watched or implied that we were always trying to pull something. The last question that was asked was about the possibility of hiring two people to fill vacancies that had been open for several months. We got another chuckle and an answer about how hiring two people would make life pretty easy for all of us when there wasn't any type of emergency.

By that time, the two supervisors had put down the markers and were just standing by the easels, looking real uncomfortable.

I looked around. Everybody had their arms folded across

their chest and were staring at the floor. The meeting ended pretty quickly after that.

(County employee)

THE TREE OF BLAME

Doubt within organizations is one of the natural by-products of the traditional organizational chart that the early industrial giants adapted from the military model.

These charts show reporting relationships in a descending order of power and delineate functional areas of responsibility within an organization.

While it can't be faulted for its ability to identify reporting relationships, the traditional organizational chart often proves the validity of its nickname, the "tree of blame." Here's how it works: Something goes wrong within an organization and immediately each level of power, as outlined on the chart, looks to the one below it in an effort to place blame. Of course, this same procedure isn't followed when something good occurs.

The newspaper I work for is located in a town with a population of about 40,000. It is within driving distance of a city of more than a million. Our major competition comes from their morning and evening papers, as well as *USA Today*, which is delivered to homes each morning by carriers. For years we had maintained a healthy subscription base by featuring local news and events of interest not covered elsewhere.

When the longtime editor retired, the publisher unexpectedly went outside and hired a replacement from an eastern newspaper, which was located in a city about four times our size. From day one, things began to change. We were told that our paper was going to become more like a big city paper. There would be less emphasis on the local scene and better coverage of national and world events.

I won't bore you with all the details, but as circulation dropped, first the advertising manager was fired because advertising revenue had plummeted. Next the circulation manager was let go because subscriptions were falling.

It took two years, but finally the publisher fired the editor, blaming all of our financial problems on him. The publisher is still here, and he still talks about the mistakes that 'they' made that almost put us out of business.

(Newspaper sports editor)

In the organization that operates with an atmosphere of doubt and mistrust, employees find an organizational chart useful for one thing: It helps them to avoid wandering into the demilitarized zones that separate "us" from "them," one functional department from another.

Doubt about an employee's intentions often grows geometrically when he or she is found in another department asking for help or advice from the employee of another supervisor.

I was on my way out of the plant when I decided to stop by the scheduling department to see if we would be running line #3 the next day. I got my answer and headed home.

The next morning, my boss called me in and started giving me the third degree about being in the office. He told me from now on to come to him with my questions. Later, I found out that the guy I talked to in scheduling got chewed out by his boss, who then called my boss in production and raised hell about me.

What's that old saying, 'We have met the enemy, and they is us'? No wonder there is tension around this place.

(Plant foreman)

THE ACTIONS OF ONE CAN AFFECT MANY

Some employees aren't worthy of the trust and freedom they are given on the job. Such employees do a real disservice to their peers since their actions may cause doubts that

have repercussions on those who have operated in a trustworthy manner.

> The people who work for me are provided company cars for
> company business. They drive their own cars to and from
> work. One day, I got a call from one of the company's me-
> chanics. He told me that one of my employees just called him
> from a small town about 50 miles away. He had the company
> car and something had happened to the transmission and he
> couldn't get it in reverse. Well, we had to have the car towed
> back to work. My employee was out of our service area when
> this happened and when I questioned him about it he told me
> he was on company business and just made a short side trip to
> save himself from having to go after work. I checked out his
> story and found out that he did have an appointment about 11
> miles away from where he had car trouble. He admitted he
> was wrong and said it wouldn't happen again. Ever since
> then, I know I check on all of my employees more than I used
> to. Maybe I was naive to think everyone would play by the
> rules.
>
> (Division manager)

The division manager assumed a level of maturity and
responsibility in all of his employees that was not true for
at least one of them. His reaction of initially checking on all
of his employees was normal. However, his doubt caused
him to *continue* checking on everyone, and this could easily
lead to a deterioration in his relationship with his people.
At first, those people were probably upset with the employee who caused the problem. Later, when the checking
continued even though there was no reason for it, they
probably began to resent being treated as if they had done
something wrong.

Thus, the ability of the division manager to evaluate
each employee individually and to tailor his relationship
with each one accordingly will be critical to the future relationship of this work group.

SUSPICION AND DOUBT CAN ERODE A RELATIONSHIP

A relationship, whether it be personal or work-based, can survive many ups and downs so long as neither party does anything to cause the other to develop suspicion or doubt about the integrity of the relationship. Once something causes a loss of trust and confidence, it becomes very difficult to restore that relationship to its original status.

Since Lynn and I were the two highest-paid women in the organization, it was natural for us to develop a special relationship even though she was one level higher than I. We were the only women that attended the regular management meetings and the only ones to be part of the top management team that went to a resort for a two-day planning retreat every fall.

Because of her position as the company's chief financial officer and mine as manager of human resources, we worked together on some projects, like costing out the proposals on union contracts and calculating the annualized cost of the benefits package.

One of those benefits was health insurance, which our company had always made available to the retired employees and their spouses at the employees' expense. Even though we didn't pay the premiums, their claims were included in the overall cost of our plan. This group's claims annually represented a disproportionate share of the total claims and total cost of our company's healthplan.

When our company received a letter detailing a 19 percent increase in health insurance annual premiums, Dave, our CEO, asked Lynn and me to study the data to see if we felt that the increase was justified. He also asked that we make any recommendations that we felt were appropriate.

Our analysis showed that a major portion of the increase had been caused by the claims of our retired employees. We discussed the pros and cons of recommending that the retired employees be placed in a separate group so that their costs would affect only their rates. During the conversation, I made what I admit was a flippant remark that, if the coverage wasn't available, the retired employees would be forced to evaluate other plans, which could result in saving all of us money. We agreed that wasn't going to happen since Dave strongly supported the present setup.

A few days later, before we had finalized recommendations, I was called into Dave's office. I received a dressing down for having such little regard for our retired employees. It finally came out that Lynn had told Dave that if it were left up to me, we wouldn't even offer hospitalization coverage to our retirees. I tried to explain, but Dave was upset and wouldn't listen to me.

When I asked Lynn why she had told Dave about our conversation, she acted as if I had suggested the elimination of insurance for retired employees.

Our conversation got me nowhere, but it did point out that I would be foolish to let my guard down again when working with Lynn.

(Manager of human resources)

BUILDING BETTER WORK RELATIONSHIPS

The leader plays a key role in eliminating suspicions and doubts in the workplace. Openness and acceptance begin with the attitude that is projected. Every action or reaction, every look or gesture conveys an open or a closed point of view.

Do you remember this old story?

A person moved to a new town and asked one of the residents, "What are the people in this town like?" The resident said, "What were the people like in the town you just left?" The new person answered, "They were unfriendly and nasty." And the town resident answered, "I think you'll find the people here just about the same."

Later, the same resident was approached by another new arrival, who asked the same question. Again, the resident asked, "What were the people like in the town you just left?" The answer was that the people were, "warm and friendly." And the resident answered, "I think you'll find the people here just about the same."

The point is, if you believe that people are untrustworthy and must be watched, you can expect to find those kinds of people wherever you work, and your attitude will convey these negative feelings. On the other hand, if you believe that people basically have the same drives and level of ambition that you have, you'll probably find those kinds of people in any company you work for during your career.

You cannot be assured that your attitude alone will eliminate suspicion among your employees, but you should never underestimate the influence you have in establishing the prevailing atmosphere in the workplace.

Taking Stock

Instructions: For each statement, circle the number that most closely represents how often that statement is true for you. Use the following as a guide:

Almost never	Seldom	Occasionally	Frequently	Usually	Almost always
0	1	2	3	4	5

1. Are you suspicious of your employees' motives?   0   1   2   3   4   5
2. Do you expect your employees to look out for themselves in most situations?   0   1   2   3   4   5
3. Do you discourage interdepartmental efforts?   0   1   2   3   4   5
4. Do you take credit for the good things that your employees accomplish?   0   1   2   3   4   5
5. Do you believe your employees lack your drive and ambition?   0   1   2   3   4   5

Scoring

Total your scores from the five questions.

If your total score is from 18 to 25: Your workers probably lack spontaneity and are often defensive. You need to take immediate steps to build open relationships with your workers by sharing more of yourself and giving them a chance to prove themselves.

If your total score is from 9 to 17: Your workers are probably unsure of how you will react to their efforts when the "chips are down." Work on your reactions to difficult situations and openly support your employees when their efforts warrant it.

If your total score is from 0 to 8: Your employees probably feel your support and know where they stand with you under all types of conditions. Continue to expect the best from others; if one person lets you down, don't let his or her actions affect your attitude toward others.

New Beginnings

Liberating the human spirit in the workplace begins with the recognition and acknowledgment of the past practices that have caused workers to lose heart.

Far too often, no thought has been given to the individual needs of those who make up the organization. As a result, we have created anticommunities of workers, consisting of people who have learned to control their emotions, ignore their instincts, regard the actions of their co-workers with suspicion, and perpetuate interdepartmental rivalries and feuds.

We can do better!

Some organizations are already well into this process.

The key is effective leadership, leadership that is capable of seeking success for the organization while recognizing the individuality and freedom of each employee.

II

THE PROCESS: CHANGING THE OPERATING ENVIRONMENT

Employees need to feel they play an important part in a team effort. Leaders recognize that others work with them, not for them, and they encourage teamwork by creating an open and inclusive atmosphere.

Chapter 3

Creating a Positive Environment

There are leaders who recognize the imperfections of a "no-change" philosophy and the inhumanity of a demotivating environment and are working to develop an entirely different type of workplace atmosphere. These individuals are willing to challenge the status quo and accept the risks of operating in ways that fly in the face of management approaches that cause broken spirits. They encourage collaboration among workers and recognize that their job is to *free* others so that they can excel.

These leaders operate with a set of beliefs that are very different from the beliefs practiced by managers who see *control* as the primary job of anyone with authority.

The following is a comparison of some of these beliefs:

Old Beliefs	New Beliefs
In every situation, there will be winners and losers.	Situations can result in everyone's winning.
All ideas come from management.	Everyone needs to be encouraged to share his or her ideas.
Fear is a great motivator.	Recognition is a great motivator.
All that workers are interested in is money.	Workers and managers have similar interests.
Only tell workers what you have to.	Share all information that isn't confidential.
Get results through intimidation.	Get results through shared responsibility.
Treat every employee the same.	Recognize the uniqueness of each person.
Work is serious business.	Work is a part of life—have a good time.

An operating philosophy based on concepts such as these new beliefs helps to create the type of environment in which motivated employees can thrive.

I've been with this company for 21 years, and I've had just two bosses. The first one retired about three years ago. He was one of those kind of guys who liked to take credit for everything good that ever happened in our division. In situations where he wasn't even involved, he would say things like, 'It wasn't easy, but we managed to overcome that problem.'

He also had a habit of keeping information from us. He would say, 'I'll fill you in as soon as the information is for general distribution.' Whenever he would say something like that, we usually could ask somebody else in management and find out that the information wasn't even confidential.

When he retired, we got a boss who is just the opposite. He isn't afraid to tell us when we do a good job, and he also gives us the credit when his boss comes around.

He's also great on sharing information and keeping us informed. He asks for our opinions and he jokes around with us.

I keep expecting to get the news that he has been promoted out of our division. When he is, he'll go with my good wishes. He deserves to move on up.

My only hope is that there is another good one out there someplace. It would be rough to go back to those old ways again."

(Foreman)

Leaders are constantly looking for ways to add to their personal list of beliefs in order to create a more motivating environment. In doing so, they look for answers to questions such as these:

- What do workers want from their jobs?
- How can our work environment be improved?
- What things am I doing that are stifling my employees?

A good place to begin your own research for answers to these types of questions is with the works of Frederick

Herzberg, who devoted many years to the study of motivation. Beginning in the late 1950s, Herzberg presented a two-factor theory that addressed questions like the ones listed above. Herzberg interviewed employees who were asked to recall work-related situations that caused their positive feelings about their job to either increase or decrease.

Based upon these answers, Herzberg concluded that the job factors that resulted in positive feelings (and job satisfaction) were different from those that caused negative feelings (and job dissatisfaction). In a 1968 issue of the *Harvard Business Review*, Herzberg presented an article entitled, "One more time: How Do You Motivate Employees?" In that article, Herzberg says:

> The opposite of job satisfaction is not job dissatisfaction but, rather, *no* job satisfaction; and, similarly, the opposite of job dissatisfaction is not job satisfaction, but *no* job dissatisfaction. Stating the concept presents a problem in semantics, for we normally think of satisfaction and dissatisfaction as opposites—i.e., what is not satisfying must be dissatisfying, and vice versa. But when it comes to understanding the behavior of people in their jobs, more than a play on words is involved.
>
> Two different needs of man are involved here. One set of needs can be thought of as stemming from his animal nature—the built-in drive to avoid pain from the environment, plus all the learned drives which become conditioned to the basic biological needs. For example, hunger, a basic biological drive, makes it necessary to earn money and then money becomes a specific drive. The other set of needs relates to that unique human characteristic, the ability to achieve and, through achievement, to experience psychological growth. The stimuli for the growth needs are tasks that induce growth; in the industrial setting, they are the *job content*. Contrariwise, the stimuli inducing pain-avoiding behavior are found in the *job environment*.

Herzberg then classifies these two types of factors as follows:

1. The **growth** or **motivator factors.**

   Achievement.

   Recognition for work well done.

   Responsibility.

   Interesting and challenging work.

   The opportunity for advancement.

Herzberg states that these are the intrinsic elements within the content of the job that are the primary cause of personal motivation and satisfaction.

He contends that while the presence of these factors increases personal motivation and job satisfaction, their absence does not create dissatisfaction. Rather, employees will not be satisfied and may not be motivated.

2. The **dissatisfiers** or **hygiene factors.**

   Interpersonal relationships.

   Company policies.

   Status.

   Pay.

   Working conditions.

   Job security and benefits.

   Supervision.

Herzberg's view is that these factors are not an intrinsic part of the job but are related to the work environment and the conditions under which the job is performed. He maintains that if these factors are positive, they will not increase a worker's satisfaction with the job, but if they are viewed as negative, they will cause job dissatisfaction and reduce the motivation to perform.

Herzberg's two-factor theory has provided the basis for many job-enrichment programs and offers many answers to the questions posed earlier.

For example, if you are searching for answers to the question, "What do workers want from their jobs?" look to

Herzberg's motivator factors. These are the items that employees will respond to in a positive way. They want to make a real contribution to the success of the company; they appreciate a pat on the back for a job well done; they like to use their own judgment and to have the opportunity to make decisions; they want the opportunity to learn more, and they appreciate job challenges; and they want to be considered when there are opportunities for advancement that are within their scope of abilities.

To answer the question, "How can our work environment be improved?" review Herzberg's Hygiene Factors and do the things necessary so that your employees will view these factors in a positive way. Reducing negative feelings about these factors will reduce job dissatisfaction among your employees.

With regard to the third question, "What things am I doing that are stifling my employees?" evaluate yourself in terms of the old and new beliefs presented at the beginning of this chapter. If you have to admit to yourself that you identify with any of the old beliefs, you can be sure that you are stifling your employees and that changes are in order.

OVER FORTY YEARS OF GOOD ADVICE

Frederick Herzberg is just one of many who have, over the past 40 years provided an understanding of the type of environment that must exist before cooperation can flourish in the workplace.

As early as the 1950s, the writings of Peter Drucker provided managers and supervisors with basic and practical guidelines. In the 1960s, we were given several new approaches. In addition to the works of Herzberg, there were novel and exciting new workplace concepts presented by Douglas McGregor, Robert Tannenbaum, and several others. The 1970s saw Paul Hersey and Ken Blanchard build on the available information to provide new insights into the variety of styles that an effective leader must use on the job. In the 1980s, Tom Peters drew a clear distinction between the role of manager as "cop" and that of leader as "cheerleader."

In this decade, we have been able to turn to the visionary works of such authors as Max DePree, Peter Block, and Peter Senge for modern insights into ways to humanize the workplace through leaders who assume new roles as stewards, servants, and teachers.

Therefore, since the 1950s, there has been a fairly continuous stream of new concepts available to the individual seeking new ways to approach the task of leading others. These concepts reflect a changing workplace and a corresponding change in the type of leader behavior that is needed to successfully balance customer, organization, and employee needs. Some of the ways that the American work scene has changed are highlighted below.

	1950s	*1990s*
Management style	"Just do what you're told."	"Let's solve this together."
Quality of product or service	Low quality	High quality
View of the customer	"Take it or leave it."	"Without you, we cannot exist."
View of employees	"A cost of doing business."	"Our most important asset."

ENCOURAGING WORKER INVOLVEMENT

With all of this available information and the dramatic changes that have occurred in the workplace, there are some managers and supervisors who still place too much emphasis on control.

There is a strong connection between *being responsible* and *being in control* that most of us have experienced early in life. We grew up being accountable to others who also controlled many of our actions. These included parents, teachers, and coaches. For example, our parents, being responsible for our safety, controlled when we crossed the street, what we ate, and whom we played with.

By the time we find ourselves in a work role that requires us to be responsible for the actions of others, it is natural to implement a control system that is consistent with what we have experienced in our own life. Thus it wouldn't be unusual to delegate work and then closely control how it is done.

Breaking the connection between responsibility and control is difficult enough. Building a connection between responsibility and freedom, which is what is advocated in this book, is even more difficult for many to comprehend. Ultimately, it requires an understanding that caring about another's well-being is more clearly reflected in a relationship that is built on freedom rather than control.

What I am advocating is the development of work relationships that do not require any of the participants to relinquish their identity in the process.

In a successful marriage, both parties retain their own identities, and together the couple builds a mutual identity that reflects their uniqueness as partners in a relationship.

In a lesser way, work relationships should reflect the same kind of individual identity retention and the building of mutual identities.

Whether it be in a marriage or any other type of relationship, individual freedom is the key to developing these kinds of associations.

Much of the remainder of this book deals with the ways you can build new relationships with your employees and liberate them from outdated control methods.

Taking Stock

Instructions: For each statement, circle the number that most closely represents how often that statement is true for you. Use the following as a guide:

Almost never 0	*Seldom* 1	*Occasionally* 2	*Frequently* 3	*Usually* 4	*Almost always* 5

1. Do you believe that you get better results from employees if you closely control them?		0 1 2 3 4 5
2. Do you believe that fear is a great motivator?		0 1 2 3 4 5
3. Do you believe that workers are only interested in money?		0 1 2 3 4 5
4. Do you tell employees only what they need in order to do the job?		0 1 2 3 4 5
5. Do you care whether your employees are stifled by their work environment?		0 1 2 3 4 5

Scoring

Total your scores from the five questions.

If your total score is from 18 to 25: Your employees probably feel left out of things and often compete with one another in a controlled and somber environment. You need to accept the blame for creating an unacceptable work environment. Only you can make the necessary changes that will allow your employees to experience personal motivation and job satisfaction.

If your total score is from 9 to 17: Your employees are probably guarded around you and wonder why you are so inconsistent. Be conscious of your tendency to mix up motivator and hygiene factors.

If your total score is from 0 to 8: Your employees probably feel that their efforts are appreciated and are eager to prove that your faith in them is deserved. Continue to build an effective team by utilizing the motivator factors and encouraging cooperation.

Chapter 4

Fostering Mutual Respect

Mutual respect in the workplace results from time spent together working on matters of common interest, which allows each party to acquire an appreciation of the other's gifts and abilities.

Leaders recognize that no one person has all of the answers. They realize that, *all* of us can develop a better approach than any *one* of us.

It seems logical to assume that the team approach to solving problems and working together would be universally practiced. Unfortunately, that is not the case. While there are leaders who have used this approach for years, there are also many managers and supervisors who have operating philosophies that reflect little regard for the abilities of a majority of their employees.

REVISITING THE PAST

It's been nearly 35 years since Douglas McGregor wrote *The Human Side of Enterprise,* in which he discussed some traditional assumptions that organizations hold about their workers and contrasted these views with a more contemporary look at the worker of that time.

McGregor suggested that managerial decisions and actions are affected by the assumptions that are made about people. He then listed three major assumptions he felt were representative of the traditional views of management, which he labeled Theory X:

1. The average human being has a built-in dislike for work and will avoid it or do as little of it as possible.
2. Because of this dislike for work, most people must be forced, controlled, threatened, or closely supervised to get them to put forth an acceptable level of effort toward the achievement of organizational objectives.
3. The average human being has little ambition, prefers to be directed in order to avoid responsibility, and is mainly interested in his own security.

Later, McGregor listed some key assumptions he felt represented the newer attitudes in dealing with people. He referred to these as Theory Y:

1. The average human being does not have a built-in dislike for work.
2. People will exercise self-direction and self-control to accomplish objectives to which they are committed.
3. People are eager to learn in order to grow and develop professionally.
4. People are motivated by things that challenge them or are of interest to them.
5. The capacity to utilize a high degree of imagination and creativity in the solution of organizational problems is widely distributed in the population.
6. People want to contribute to the success of their organization.

Douglas McGregor's ideas have implications that are as far-reaching today as they were in the 1960s. Assumptions that managers make about workers still influence work-related decisions and either promote or block the development of mutual respect.

In the narration that follows, note how differently a Theory X-style person and a Theory Y-style person view the same situation.

Our company has been in business for over 50 years. During all that time, it has used some type of time clock and time card system for the hourly employees. Recently, discussions began about eliminating this system. Ron, our plant superintendent, was strongly opposed to doing away with the existing system, while Pat, the director of support services, favored the move. Others had opinions, but no one was as directly involved as Ron and Pat, so they had become the informal leaders of the two factions.

After two meetings, no one had shown any inclination to budge on his or her opinion. The general manager wanted a decision. He called a third—and what he said would be the last—meeting. He told everyone to be prepared to talk the matter through and to plan on leaving the meeting with a decision.

At the meeting, he recognized Ron and Pat as the leaders of two groups that were poles apart in their thinking. He asked each one to list the three top reasons why his or her point of view should be adopted.

Ron went first and wrote the following three reasons on the board:

1. The system has worked for over 50 years. We have been able to keep track of people since they have to clock in and out.

2. People know that if they are late they will get docked, so the time clock keeps them honest.

3. If we do away with this system, we are inviting people to take advantage of us.

Pat then listed her three reasons:

1. Our people are just as trustworthy as those in any other company, and these kinds of systems have disappeared in companies that trust their people and want to make a statement to that effect.

2. We are wasting time and money keeping track of people who deserve to be treated just like all of us who don't clock in now.

3. If we have to rely on a time clock to control people, we are in real trouble.

Everyone studied the two lists for a few minutes and then people started discussing how to do away with the time clock.

Finally, Ron spoke up. He said, "Everyone's acting like a decision has been made."

The general manager answered, "I think it has, Ron."

The meeting concluded with an outline of how we would proceed.

(Personnel director)

The Theory X approach to dealing with people blocks the development of mutual respect. It excludes the concept of mutuality from a boss–subordinate situation and is an integral part of a top-down, hierarchical approach that blocks employee involvement in the workplace. The Theory X approach promotes *control* of the worker.

On the other hand, the Theory Y approach encourages mutual respect because the employee is viewed as having the same inherent values as the manager. Therefore, employee involvement is taken for granted because the manager's assumptions about other people are based on positives, such as the six items listed earlier. This forms a strong basis for the development of a relationship in which the Theory Y type manager will seek ways to *free* the worker to perform in creative and meaningful ways.

THE RELATIONSHIP BETWEEN THEORY Y AND EMPOWERMENT

One approach to modernizing McGregor's works involves discussing whether employees are "empowered" to contribute to the organization's success in a meaningful way. Although "empowered" has become overused of late, there is a clear relationship between the treatment afforded to employees by the Theory Y-style leader and the empowering leader. They both hold their employees in high esteem and value them as instrumental to the organization's overall success. Both instill within their people a sense of belonging and the knowledge that they are important and respected for who and what they are.

Both of these concepts are founded on respect for the uniqueness, individuality, and value of each and every person.

A CRISIS MAY LEAD TO NEW UNDERSTANDINGS

When a company is in trouble, the management may, for the first time, turn to its employees for help. As a consequence of the contacts that result, managers often come to some new understandings. For instance, they discover that their employees have families, that they have dreams and aspirations for themselves and their kids, that they have sick parents or parents that die unexpectedly, that there are times when they want to brag about something in their personal lives, and that there are times they wish there was someone who would just listen.

> We were in real trouble. Sales were down, rejects and returned goods were at an all-time high. Every top-management meeting turned into a bitch session about our production employees. Finally we called in a consultant. We told her the facts as we saw them. She spent about a month in our plant. She talked to employees in small groups and had lots of one-on-one sessions with some of them. She was there during both shifts and had a free hand to do whatever she needed to do. Finally, she came into my office and said that she had reached some preliminary conclusions. I said, 'Good, what's our problem?' She looked me in the eye and said, 'You and your management staff are your major problem.' She then proceeded to tell me

things about my own operation that I didn't know. She finished her report by saying, 'You have many dedicated employees who have a lot at stake here. They want this company to succeed just as badly as you do. They will work with you if you will give them a chance.'

A lot has changed since then, and it wasn't all easy. Now we understand that it's not 'our problems' and 'their problems,' it's 'everybody's problems.' We are back competing, and we are doing it with the same people, and they are running the same machines we had before. It was a humbling experience to find out how many things we had been doing wrong and how much smarter our employees are than we had given then credit for.

(CEO)

Theory X managers who learn that their workers are human beings with feelings, needs, and wants, just like their own, are likely to change the assumptions that guide their ways of dealing with their employees.

WALKING IN THE OTHER PERSON'S SHOES

Another way to develop respect for others is to spend the time necessary to come to an understanding of their environment. This does not happen when management isolates itself from the problems of the organization it is responsible for.

The company announced that there was going to be an addition to our main building. About a week before construction was to begin, a chain-link fence was built around the site. As a result, what had been a 30-yard walk from our building to the main one became a 100-yard walk around the perimeter of the fence to get to the same door we had always used.

Well, bad weather set in, and the project was delayed. Five weeks later, one of the top management guys needed to come over to our building to check on something, and some of us just happened to be out front.

This guy came out and started on a straight line for our building. All of a sudden, he realized that he was blocked by the fence. He stopped, looked the situation over, and then walked around the perimeter of the fence.

When he got to our building he asked us, 'Do you have bolt cutters around here?' One of the guys, Mike, told him we did, and he asked Mike to go get them.

When Mike returned, the management guy proceeds to show him where to cut the fence so there is an opening directly between the buildings.

Construction finally got started about three weeks later, and we had to go around again, but we always remembered those weeks we walked around the fence because management either didn't know or didn't care about our being inconvenienced.

(Laborer)

THE RESULTS OF A "GOOD GUY–BAD GUY" MENTALITY

Sometimes, managerial actions and decisions are based on assumptions that are rooted in a "good guy–bad guy" outlook. In these cases, employees are categorized on the basis of some form of stereotyping, and no consideration is given to the individual. Often, an action is viewed as being "good" or "bad," "right" or "wrong," on the basis of who is involved rather than on the merits of the action itself.

I worked for 14 years in gas line construction, and never once did I feel like the operations manager respected or trusted me. Sometimes he would walk right past me and not even acknowledge me. Then I applied for an opening in line staking, and I was awarded the job. On Friday, I was a union construction worker, and in his eyes I was nothing. On the very next Monday, I was a nonunion staking engineer, with a lot to learn, and he went out of his way to look me up and congratulate me. He even shook my hand! When it happened, I was so shocked I don't think I even said anything.

Later, when I told my wife about what happened, she put her finger right on it. She said, 'No wonder you always hated working for that jerk, and no wonder there are so many problems between the company and the union.'

(Staking engineer)

Stereotyping of individuals and groups results in splintered work relationships. It results in a form of discrimination in the workplace. The operations manager in the previous story will never be cited for discrimination, but his attitudes and beliefs are just as lethal in terms of how they affect his organization.

TO EARN RESPECT, STICK WITH THE BASICS

There are certain qualities of leadership that are basic for earning respect from others. No list can be offered as all-inclusive, but the one that follows provides a good starting point, which you can add to, based upon your own experiences.

Tell the Truth

Once discovered, a lie can irretrievably destroy credibility. If not discovered, a lie can lead to other lies. Sooner or later, others will begin to doubt you, and, even more important, you may begin to doubt yourself. If you always tell the truth, you don't have to try to remember what you told others about any situation.

Lead by Example

The leader should be the role model for acceptable performance. The late Jim Hayes, former chairman of the board of the American Management Association once wrote in

(*Memos for Management: LEADERSHIP*, New York: AMA-CON 1983):

> Leaders should lead—by example. Words may exhort but example quietly persuades and inspires. Ideally, words and example should coalesce. Consistency between words and behavior—that is, a lack of hypocrisy—steels many executives to demand the performance required by the implicit contract that underlies each employee–company relationship. If the work ethic has been in decline in American industry, then perhaps it is because those, who by their own behavior should be showing the way, have been shirking their jobs.

Employees should be able to view their leader as a role model for acceptable behavior.

- Do you tell others that it is their responsibility to get to work on time, or do you show others, through your actions, that getting to work on time is important?
- Do you tell others that they are an important part of the company or do you show up in the work area to demonstrate their importance?
- Do you tell others about the right way to do things or do you do the right things and set an example for others to follow?

In other words, do you talk a good game, or do you actually, "walk the talk"?

Provide a Vision

Regardless of how much information is shared within an organization, others need to know your slant on things. They need to have their fear of the unknown erased by your positive and inspiring vision of what lies beyond the horizon. They also need to know that you know how to proceed to meet the challenges that lie ahead.

Act Decisively

There will be times when you, and you alone, must make tough decisions. There is nothing wrong with deliberating your alternatives. However, if the matter is important enough to require your involvement, after a logical amount of time for deliberating, you will need to follow through on your decision.

Some leaders habitually procrastinate on tough decisions. One such person once told me he'd found that by waiting, many situations no longer required his involvement in the decision-making process. Such an approach is not delegation; it is abdication from one of the most important functions of leadership.

There is a saying attributed to Karl Rahner:

> A man who refuses to commit himself for fear of following an insight that cannot be mathematically verified does not in fact remain free but rather enters upon the worst of all commitments—that of living without commitment. He tries to live as a neutral, deciding nothing, and that in itself is a decision.

Not making a decision on an important matter does not mean nothing will happen. Obviously, something will happen, even if it is nothing, when something is badly needed by the organization.

Involve Others

The participative approach works! Those closest to the problem usually have lots of ideas about how to solve it. Solicit their opinions and let them help you plan the approach that will be used. People who have been involved in the initial stages of planning are much more likely to commit their talents to seeing it accomplished.

Some leaders lament about its being lonely at the top. Some of this loneliness cannot be avoided. All aspects of the leader's role cannot and should not be shared. However, whenever it is appropriate, which will be most of the time, the leader should invite others to share in mastering difficult situations.

Develop Others

The leader works to develop the potential in others. After ensuring that people understand what their job is and are properly trained, the leader delegates duties to them, supports their efforts, gives them the opportunity to succeed and sometimes fail, and stands behind them so that they can concentrate on improvement rather than worry about retaliation.

A leader recognizes that he makes himself more promotable by giving others the capability to replace him in his present job. He also recognizes that the company is better prepared to deal with the future if it has trained, self-sufficient, and responsible employees.

Acknowledge the Accomplishments of Others

As employees grow on the job, they will experience an increasing number of successes. As these occur, it is important that the leader affirm the employees directly and also acknowledge their successes to others. Giving credit to others is a hallmark of a true leader and is a confidence builder for the developing employee.

Seek Self-Development

Leaders need to seek out new information that will help them further develop their own potential. Their curiosity about finding new and better ways of doing things is driven by the fact that they see learning as a lifetime opportunity.

RESPECT: A KEY TO BUILDING AND MAINTAINING RELATIONSHIPS

In most work situations, the effort to remove barriers that exist between workers and management must be initiated by management. The success of this effort will depend, to a great extent, upon the assumptions that management makes about its workers. Therefore, a high percentage of success stories include some change in the organization's hierarchy, which results in a positive change in these assumptions.

Leaders who are involved in this process recognize that workers may be rightfully skeptical and cautious in reacting to efforts to change the operating environment. In the face of doubt, the leader's unwavering faith in people will be instrumental to the eventual success of this process. Their respect for others makes it possible for the eventual development of mutual respect between the parties.

Leaders understand that respect, like trust and loyalty, must be earned. They recognize that once earned, respect can be damaged or lost through careless or thoughtless acts. Therefore, they work to avoid such acts.

Through a recognition of, and an appreciation for, the gifts that others possess, leaders develop a regard for others that is genuine. When this is coupled with their basic belief that others have the same internal motivators that they themselves possess, leaders are capable of developing work relationships that are built on respect.

Taking Stock

Instructions: For each statement, circle the number that most closely represents how often that statement is true for you. Use the following as a guide:

Almost never 0	Seldom 1	Occasionally 2	Frequently 3	Usually 4	Almost always 5

1. Do you believe that your employees lack motivation and require constant supervision?   0   1   2   3   4   5

2. Do all of your conversations with employees stay focused on the tasks to be accomplished?   0   1   2   3   4   5

3. Do you believe that your employees have less integrity than you do?   0   1   2   3   4   5

4. Do you believe that most of your employees prefer to avoid workplace responsibility?   0   1   2   3   4   5

5. Do you believe that your employees are incapable of providing meaningful ideas?   0   1   2   3   4   5

Scoring

Total your scores for the five questions.

If your total score is from 18 to 25: You are making "Theory X" assumptions about your workers. Only you can take the steps necessary to change the existing environment.

If your total score is from 9 to 17: Your employees probably don't react as positively as you would like. They may have given up trying to figure out how you feel about them. Work on seeing them as partners who can help solve problems.

If your total score is from 0 to 8: Your employees should feel your respect and believe that they work with you, not for you. Work to build on the existing atmosphere and continue your "Theory Y" approach.

Chapter 5

Developing Mutual Trust

If there is an attribute that can be considered the foundation in the process of building a quality relationship, it is trust.

Almost everyone has his own way of characterizing what a person would have to do to be considered trustworthy. Included in any list would be items such as: truthfulness; consistency and fairness in all actions; and an ability to handle others' vulnerabilities with tact.

There also seem to be two controlling elements with regard to trust: time and proximity. The more often you are around someone and the longer his or her behavior is consistent with your perception of a trustworthy person, the greater the trust you will place in that person.

There is no greater compliment in the relationship-building process than to be told, "I trust you." Such trust is earned, over time, by the leader who demonstrates a consistency between words and actions.

Our department got a new manager. The day she took over, she had a group meeting at headquarters with all of us present. One of the things she told us was to let her know if we needed anything that would help us do our job better.

I had been trying to get a new calculator with a paper printout capability through my old boss for over six months. He just kept telling me, 'I'll look into it.'

When the meeting with our new boss broke up, I told her I needed the calculator and I explained what I used it for.

Two days later, the machine I needed was delivered to my office. I couldn't believe it. The fact that she believed me and took some action meant a lot to me. I let the other people in the department know about it, too. It sure got us started off on the right foot.

(Engineer)

HOW YOUR ACTIONS ARE JUDGED

In the workplace, your ability to be equitable and free from bias in dealing with others becomes a critical part of their judgment about your trustworthiness. For example, if you show favoritism, you will have an extremely difficult time earning trust.

The same thing can be said about your attitude. Others can sense how you view them: If your attitude conveys doubt about their honesty and truthfulness, it is natural they will become defensive in their dealings with you. If, on the other hand, your attitude conveys that you accept them at face value, then, over time, they will feel less and less need to keep their defenses up, and the whole work atmosphere can be improved.

> The rest of us in the management group have learned that we have to be careful about what we say around George, our chief financial officer. There have been too many times that George has spent time with the CEO and afterwards, one of us found ourselves in some kind of trouble. George likes to 'confidentially' discuss company matters with each of us individually, but we've learned to keep our guards up.

(Vice president)

YOUR ACTIONS ARE GUIDED BY YOUR ASSUMPTIONS

Much has been written about the so-called Pygmalion effect. Briefly, this theory suggests that teachers, managers, and supervisors who make positive assumptions about the potential of their students or workers will act in positive ways towards them. They indicate that they not only expect good performance but that they have confidence that their people will meet or exceed these expectations. This theory also suggests that those who make negative assumptions about others' potential will act in negative ways towards them, indicating that they expect poor performance. They have little or no confidence that their people will surprise them with better-than-expected results.

There are documented examples that show high levels of performance from people about whom positive assumptions were made and poor performance by people about whom negative assumptions were made.

If you combine the ideas of Douglas McGregor with the theories contained in the Pygmalion effect, it is easy to see how opinions and assumptions can influence the work relationship.

Theory Y-type managers, who make positive assumptions about people, will consistently act in positive ways that indicate they expect good performance. They will, on an ongoing basis, exude confidence that their people are capable of a high level of performance. Typically, this type of manager will be very much at ease around his or her people. His or her attitude will normally put employees at ease because it will be consistently positive and affirming of their job performance.

I've had good bosses before, but I've never had one that had so much confidence in my abilities. For awhile, I think she believed in me more than I did, and then it began to rub off on me. Her confidence in me gave me confidence that I never had before. I found myself wanting to live up to her high expectations.

(Supervisor)

THE RELATIONSHIP BETWEEN
SELF-ESTEEM AND TRUST

Self-esteem is an appreciation and acceptance of one's own being. It is the ability to look at yourself in a way that no one else can and think, "I'm glad I'm me!" Self-esteem is one of the most important qualities of a leader. The manager that appreciates his or her own efforts has an easier time appreciating the efforts of others.

> When we have a healthy respect for ourselves, there is no limit to what we can succeed in doing. When we believe that everything is possible for us, accomplishment becomes natural.
>
> No one knows better than we what is essential for our own growth and happiness. Those who direct their own lives don't depend upon kindly gnomes or favorable alignment of the planets. They use knowledge, experience, hard work, belief in themselves, and optimism to achieve their goals.
>
> Leo Buscaglia
> (*Born For Love*)

There is a range of behavior that a manager or supervisor might exhibit on the job, depending upon the degree to which she or he has developed self-esteem. At one end of the range are people who lack self-esteem. Because of this lack of self-acceptance, they doubt their own abilities, don't appreciate themselves, and are sure that others don't appreciate them either. Trust cannot develop in this type of atmosphere.

The cowardly lion in *The Wizard of Oz* has a line that typifies the thinking of this type of person. In the scene where Dorothy, the scarecrow, and the tin man first meet the lion, Dorothy invites him to join them on the journey to Oz, so he can ask the wizard for some courage. The lion says, "Wouldn't you be embarrassed to be seen in the company of a cowardly lion? I would."

Often, the manager with low self-esteem views control as an indispensable element of the position. Like the cowardly lion, this type of person lacks courage and must make up for personal fears by trying to put fear into others. This type of manager demands conformity and makes it clear that no help is needed in decision making.

Because of the power of the position, the manager may have some amount of success in controlling others, but it will be attained at a high cost. People don't like to be controlled and resent being threatened.

Another type of manager found at this end of the range is the one who places great importance on being liked by those that she or he supervises. Because this type of manager hasn't reached a high enough level of self-acceptance, he or she turns to others for needed affirmation. Usually, these managers are procrastinators and are inconsistent in the application of rules and regulations because they will vary their approach depending upon the reactions they get.

Liz ran one of our district offices for about three years. The daily cash receipts record for her office, which we wanted by 3:00 P.M. each day, was late day after day, while all of the other offices consistently met our request.

When questioned, Liz always had an excuse. Usually, she tried to claim a high level of activity, but the records didn't support her contention. Finally, when Liz went on vacation that year, instead of allowing one of her people to fill in, we sent another office supervisor to run Liz's office for the week.

We got the receipts record on time, all five days. We also got an interesting story from Sharon, the supervisor who filled in for Liz. She said that the majority of the people in the office acted offended because she insisted that the report be done on time. A couple of them said that they would have to change their break time in order to make the deadline. Sharon told them that they would have to put the report first. One of them responded, 'Liz thinks that we are more important than a report.'

Later, one of the office people told Sharon that they could meet the deadline every day, if Liz would, 'quit letting some of the employees take advantage of her.'

We are trying to work with Liz, but I'm not sure she is going to be able to do things our way. She wants to please everyone and, as a result, she isn't pleasing anyone.

(District manager)

Regardless of the amount of success individuals with low self-esteem experience, there will be times when they must admit, at least to themselves, that they have never gotten over the self-doubts and fears that make decision making difficult and most personal encounters gut-wrenching experiences.

At the other end of the range are people who have high self-esteem. They have no problem realizing that they don't have all the answers. Furthermore, they realize they can learn a lot from others.

Secure, self-confident individuals recognize there will be both successes and failures, and each is viewed as a learning experience that can lead to further development. They evaluate failures by looking for the reasons behind each one, but they don't suffer huge swings in self-esteem because of them.

People with high self-esteem like people and like the opportunities that dealing with people present. They want to improve the methods they use to deal with others and never quit looking for learning opportunities.

In stark contrast to controlling people, they work to remove fear from the workplace. They delegate decision making, pushing it down to the most appropriate level. Planning becomes a team effort, and employees' ideas and suggestions are incorporated into the process whenever possible. Over time, honesty and openness become the norm, and mutual trust develops.

In between the ends of this range are an immeasurable number of variations. All managers have had an infinite number of experiences that affect how they think about themselves and others. Future experiences will either increase or decrease their self-esteem level. At the same time, every person the manager deals with will have experiences that contribute to how they feel about themselves and others, and they will also be constantly changing. Is it any wonder that every encounter provides new challenges to the development of trusting relationships in the workplace?

JUDGING YOUR LEVEL OF SELF-ESTEEM

At this point, if it were possible, I would share the magic formula by which you could determine your personal level of self-esteem. I know of no such formula.

In his book, *The Psychology of Self-Esteem* (New York: Bantam, 1971), Dr. Nathaniel Branden states:

> There is no value judgment more important to man—no factor more decisive in his psychological development and motivation—than the estimate he passes on himself.
>
> This estimate is ordinarily experienced by him, not in the form of a conscious, verbalized judgment, but in the form of a feeling that can be hard to isolate and identify because he experiences it constantly: it is part of every other feeling, it is involved in his every emotional response.

To seek out answers about yourself, you might want to begin with this and some of Dr. Branden's other works, such as *How to Raise Your Self-Esteem* and *Honoring the Self.*

INCONSISTENCY CAN DESTROY TRUST

It takes a long time to build a trusting relationship, but one can be destroyed very quickly. All it takes is for a person to do something that indicates there is an inconsistency between what he or she says and what he or she actually does. When this happens, doubt is created in the mind of the other party in the relationship, and there is a deterioration in the level of trust.

> I told my boss about my wife's illness, so if I started acting funny, he would know what was wrong. I asked him to keep the information confidential and he agreed to do so. The next thing I knew, it was all over the building.
>
> (Marketing representative)

> One afternoon, my boss and I were involved in a bull session and we started talking about how some people keep their personal lives private while others will talk openly about practically anything. He says, 'I've found that lots of people will let their guard down if I joke with them. I get them to relax by telling them some unimportant little incident about myself, and pretty soon they will tell me something that I know, under other circumstances, they would never have shared.'
>
> He then proceeded to give me a couple of examples, with names. I felt he was sharing very private information. I left his office wondering how many times he had pulled that trick on me. I was much more careful after that.
>
> (Department manager)

A trust that has been compromised is even more difficult to repair than it was to build in the first place. The best thing to do is to work very hard at maintaining relationships and to avoid doing the thoughtless types of things that will damage them.

DEVELOPING GUIDING PRINCIPLES

In his book, *Tough-Minded Leadership*,[1] Joe Batten has a copy of a promise the managers of the Marriott Corporation sign each year as a rededication to the principles contained in it:

I promise the members of my team:

1. To set the right example for them by my own actions in all things.

2. To be consistent in my temperament so that they know how to 'read' me and what to expect from me.

3. To be fair, impartial, and consistent in matters relating to work rules, discipline, and rewards.

4. To show a sincere, personal interest in them as individuals without becoming overly 'familiar.'

5. To seek their counsel on matters that affect their jobs and to be guided as much as possible by their judgment.

6. To allow them as much individuality as possible in the way their jobs are performed, as long as the quality of the end result is not compromised.

7. To make sure they always know in advance what I expect from them in the way of conduct and performance on the job.

8. To be appreciative of their efforts and generous in praise of their accomplishments.

9. To use every opportunity to teach them how to do their jobs better and how to help themselves advance in skill level and responsibility.

10. To show them that I can 'do' as well as 'manage' by pitching in to work beside them when my help is needed.

Signed_____

---

[1] Reprinted, with permission of the publisher, from TOUGH-MINDED LEADERSHIP by Joe D. Batten, © 1989 AMACOM, a division of the American Management Association. All rights reserved.

The signed copy is returned to headquarters and is placed in the manager's personnel file.

This an outstanding list. Followed faithfully, these 10 items would go a long way in developing consistency and respect. Also, the idea of reviewing the list annually and recommitting to its contents is noteworthy. Too often, this type of list ends up in a drawer, forgotten and meaningless as far as having any impact on a person's performance. Joe Batten states that Marriott credits much of its success to basing decisions on the principles contained in this list.

Your company may not have such a list or any type of annual rededication to a set of guiding principles. But there is no reason you can't develop one. Your own list could provide a stable basis for your actions, in the same way as the Marriott organization's does.

TRUSTING OTHERS AND BEING TRUSTWORTHY YOURSELF

Most managers and supervisors would like to believe they are trusted by their employees, but this trust cannot be demanded or ordered. It must be earned through the day-to-day activities that take place on the job.

> You can buy a man's time; you can buy his physical presence at a given place; you can even buy a measured number of his skilled muscular motions per hour. But you cannot buy enthusiasm—you cannot buy initiative—you cannot buy loyalty—you cannot buy the devotion of hearts, minds or souls. You must *earn* these.
>
> Clarence Francis

Leaders who tell the truth, who are willing to share their thoughts and ideas, and who show a genuine interest in the

well-being of those they work with, can help build work relationships that are based upon mutual trust. Such relationships are one of the keys to people's working together
in harmony.

Taking Stock

Instructions: For each statement, circle the number that most closely represents how often that statement is true for you. Use the following as a guide:

Almost never 0	Seldom 1	Occasionally 2	Frequently 3	Usually 4	Almost always 5

1. Do you find it difficult to make tough decisions and often wish that someone else would do that part of your job ?   0 1 2 3 4 5
2. Do you show favoritism in your people decisions?   0 1 2 3 4 5
3. Have you learned that it is best to expect poor performance from most employees?   0 1 2 3 4 5
4. Do you wish you knew a magic formula that would cause your employees to like you more?   0 1 2 3 4 5
5. Do you believe that your employees owe you their loyalty because of your position?   0 1 2 3 4 5

Scoring

Total your scores for the five questions.

> *If your total score is from 18 to 25:* Your employees are probably close-mouthed around you. When you ask them questions, they may be evasive and reticent. Work on developing a consistency between your words and actions. You will have to take the initiative if matters are going to improve.

> *If your total score is from 9 to 17:* Because of your inconsistency, your employees probably try to avoid you. They may be uncomfortable in your presence. You will have to spend the time to repair your credibility by following through in a consistent manner and by asking for their input on matters that affect them.

> *If your total score is from 0 to 8:* Your employees probably are confident and comfortable around you. Don't take your success in building respect for granted. On the contrary, continue to be sensitive to situations that could damage the present balance.

Chapter 6

Improving the Communication Process

The successful leader realizes there is nothing more important in a relationship than honest, open, two-way communication. Being a leader includes caring enough to have a genuine interest in what others think and feel. It also includes anticipating what others want to know about the organization and providing that information on a regular basis.

DON'T KEEP SECRETS THAT AREN'T SECRETS

Too often, individuals who have access to information about the organization withhold even nonconfidential items from others. They understand that knowledge is power, that withholding information increases their ability to *control* others, and that it increases the mystique about their position within the organization.

One day at lunch, I heard a couple of employees from another department talking about the fact that the company was going to offer everyone a 401(k) plan. I asked them where they had gotten the information. They told me that their boss had told them after the last monthly staff meeting. I went back to my department and asked my boss about it. He said it was true.

When I asked him why he hadn't told us about it, he said that he didn't like to share 'newsy' items too quickly because he didn't want top management to get the idea he couldn't keep his mouth shut. Then I asked him if it was supposed to be confidential. He just looked at me, and then he said, 'I've learned that it's better to treat all information as if it were confidential.'

(Secretary)

PROVIDING NEEDED INFORMATION

When asked, employees indicate it is important for them to feel as though they are in on things that will have an impact on their job or on the company. Almost everyone within an organization has questions that need to be periodically addressed, if there is to be good relations and open communication. These include:

How Is the Organization Doing?

The longer someone is with an organization, the more interested she or he becomes in its success. Most employees want to know where the organization is going and how it plans to get there. Sure, it is a matter of job security, but it is also an indication of involvement and personal commitment.

Some organizations anticipate this interest and provide pertinent information to their employees on a regular basis.

Once a year, the company has a meeting with all of the employees in each plant. They call these meetings, 'The Annual Report to the Employees Meetings.' They use slides and have handouts that tell us how we are doing at our plant and how the company is doing overall.

What I like is that they don't try to slant things. They just give us the facts. After they finish their report, we get a chance to ask questions. Sometimes these questions get pretty pointed, but I'll give the management people credit—they have always been direct with their answers. I can't speak for everyone, but the people I work with look forward to these meetings.

(Factory worker)

Other organizations foster an atmosphere of secrecy and provide little or no information to their employees. This approach encourages the existence of an active grapevine, which may become more and more sophisticated as higher levels of employees have to resort to its use.

Such a system, once it's highly developed, can rival any formal communication process because of the ingenuity of its users, who will even utilize the company's own communication network to send and receive information.

The biggest problem with any type of informal information system is that it will be right often enough to build credibility with its users. Then, when it is wrong, serious damage may be done to the company in general or to specific individuals.

We posted a supervisor's job internally, expecting several people to apply. Five days later, we had only two applicants. We knew something wasn't right, so we started asking some questions. We found out that everyone was anticipating the posting and that about a week before it went up, someone saw Jim, one of our present supervisors, talking privately to Ron, one of the guys who ended up bidding. The word went out that the company was interested in Ron and had even talked to him privately about the job. This convinced some good candidates that they would be wasting their time to apply for the job. The conversation was actually about a situation at the local high school, which was of interest to Ron and Jim, since both have children attending there.

When we discussed the situation, we realized we had a real problem. Ron was one of the strong candidates for the supervisor's job, regardless of who else asked to be considered. If we proceeded with just two candidates and then chose Ron, it would appear as though it was, in fact, a done deal and that we were playing games in even posting the job. Of course it would also add to the credibility of the grapevine. If we somehow tried to put out the word that no deal had been cut, in an effort to attract other candidates, we would be creating a situation that would make it difficult, if not impossible, to fairly consider Ron, plus we could easily offend Ron and Jerry, the second candidate.

The whole time we discussed the situation, we got more upset about the problem that one person had caused by jumping to a conclusion and then spreading a rumor throughout the organization.

(Human resource manager)

Companies in crisis often share in-depth information with their employees. Sometimes, a crisis situation is the first time the company feels the need to level with the folks who make their product or sell their service and who have a lot at stake if the company should fail. The message may well be that things aren't going well and we need your help. Although the response from the employees may be positive, how much better it would have been for the company to share information on a regular basis and to develop a positive relationship in better times.

How Am I Doing?

If supervisors and managers would tell others the things they want and need to know about their job performance, life in the workplace would be much simpler. We tell our workers that we need good performers and that good performance will be rewarded, and then we fail to tell them whether they are doing OK, or what they could do to become a better performer.

As usual, I was nervous when it was time for my annual performance appraisal. I felt that I had put in a pretty good year, and I expected my supervisor to acknowledge my effort and to give me an increase that was at least a little above the average.

He started out by telling me that I had done a lot of good things during the year but that overall he was disappointed in several things. At that point, he pulled out a tablet and began to discuss items that he had listed chronologically. The first thing he brought up was a phone conversation of mine that he had overheard just a few days after my last appraisal. He commented on my tone of voice, which he said was 'unfriendly.' The next two items concerned personal phone calls that he said I had made. Again, the dates mentioned were almost a year old. I told him I couldn't remember any of these incidents, and then I asked him why he hadn't said something at the time. 'I have too much to do to spend my time correcting every little thing that you do,' he answered. I was thinking to myself, 'Sure, but you had time to write a note about what happened,' but I knew enough not to say anything, especially in an appraisal.

He went on through his list, making comments about situations, most of which I couldn't even remember.

When he finished, he gave me an increase that was below the average and said that he hoped I would take our conversation to heart and try to show some improvement in my performance in the coming year.

I left the appraisal disappointed and upset. By the time I thought the whole situation through, I was mad as hell and completely frustrated. I wanted to go back and see my boss and ask him how I could ever improve if he didn't take the time to talk about things right when they happen? I decided that I knew what he would say, so I just went back to work, feeling pretty helpless.

(Office worker)

To give people a chance to be top performers do the following.

Explain to Each Employee What His or Her Job Is and How That Job Is to Be Done.   Too often, employees don't receive enough information to fully understand what they are expected to accomplish.

In *Out of the Crisis* (Cambridge: MIT Press, 1986), W. Edwards Deming states:

> The production worker in America is under handicaps that are taking a terrific toll in quality, productivity, and competitive position. Barriers and handicaps rob the hourly worker of his birthright, the right to be proud of his work, the right to do a good job. These barriers exist in almost every plant, factory, company, department store, and government office in the United States today.
>
> How can anyone on the factory floor take pride in his work when he is not sure what is acceptable workmanship, and what is not, and can not find out? Right yesterday; wrong today. What is my job?

It is the leader's responsibility to ensure that every worker knows what his or her job is, how that job is to be accomplished, and exactly what is expected on a daily basis.

Give Employees Feedback on Performance While Reinforcing the Need for Effort and Improvement.   Most employees will respond positively to constructive criticism, especially when it is presented in a nonthreatening manner that recognizes their efforts, praises their improvement, and presents reasons why an alternative method might be better. An even greater number of employees will respond to being told they are doing a good job so long as they recognize that this praise is given honestly.

Work with Employees to Establish Attainable, but Challenging, Goals.   We all need to be challenged to reach new heights. New goals may seek improved quality, increased quantity, revised methods, or a combination of factors.

To gain employees' commitment, goals should be established through a dialogue process in which the employees are encouraged to express opinions and otherwise fully participate.

Remove Obstacles That Impede Progress and Stay Involved So Employees Know You Care about How They Are Doing.   As employees mature, they will accept more responsibility for their day-to-day activities but will require enough involvement from their supervisor to know there is a continuing interest in their well-being. The better the communication process, the easier it will be to know how well things are going. The supervisor will also be needed to smooth out the rough spots when they crop up.

Reward Good Performance and Recognize Accomplishments.   Top performers, who help make their company a success, should share in the financial benefits that result from this success and should receive the accolades they deserve. When it is possible and appropriate, recognize employee accomplishments publicly and be sure to give credit where credit is due. No employee likes to feel someone else is receiving credit for his or her ideas or effort.

THE CASE FOR LISTENING

Some managers and supervisors are better at the telling part of communications than they are at the listening part. Certainly, there are a lot of times when it is necessary for the person in charge to give orders and direct the activities of others. However, open communication requires that all parties have the opportunity to be listened to. Also, one of the ways employees judge how much you value them is by how attentively you listen to them.

The higher you go in an organization, the less you are required to listen to others in order to find out what you are supposed to do and when you are supposed to do it. However, the higher you go in an organization, the more you should listen to others—not to receive orders but to stay in touch and to get facts you no longer know about firsthand.

We all need to become better listeners. Unfortunately, most of us tend to jump to conclusions when someone else is doing the talking. As soon as we believe we understand what the other person is saying, we quit listening. Often, we are already thinking about how we will respond and therefore fail to listen to the complete incoming message. The only way to overcome this tendency is to stay focused when someone else is talking to us. It takes practice to become a good listener.

My wife and I have four children, all of whom are raised. One evening years ago, after a day of work, I was reading the newspaper. At the same time, one of my children, who had just started to attend school, was telling me about some adventure he had experienced that day. Every now and then I was throwing in a "mmmm" or a "that's nice."

Finally, my child said, "Daddy, are you listening to me?" "Of course," I answered. He looked at me and asked, "Then what did I say?"

All these years later, I can remember how I felt at that moment, and how I struggled to get out of that one.

After that incident, I tried to be a better listener when any of my kids was telling me something that was important to them and therefore deserved my attention.

Much of the average workday is spent in the exchange of information and ideas. I often wonder what would happen if, in the middle of a typical business conversation, I would ask a fellow worker, "Are you listening to me?" and if, when he or she said yes, I would say, "Tell me what I've been saying."

There are times when I become aware that I'm not giving another person my undivided attention in the way that I should. When this happens, I take steps to get actively involved. This includes asking questions, repeating what the other person has just said, and asking for clarification.

A big part of an effective communication process is being a good listener, and this part of the process is often neglected.

THE IMPORTANCE OF STAYING IN TOUCH

The weekly television program, "20-20," signs off with, "We're in touch, so you stay in touch." That would be a good motto for any business to consistently apply to its employees, suppliers, and customers. Keeping everyone informed and, at the same time, remaining open to hear both good news and bad would go a long way towards establishing the type of comfortable atmosphere that is needed in a competitive business.

Taking Stock

Instructions: For each statement, circle the number that most closely represents how often that statement is true for you. Use the following as a guide:

Almost never 0	*Seldom* 1	*Occasionally* 2	*Frequently* 3	*Usually* 4	*Almost always* 5

1. Do you feel a sense of power when you withhold information from your employees?   0   1   2   3   4   5
2. Do you believe that all employees need to know are the specifics of their jobs?   0   1   2   3   4   5
3. Do you feel that if you had more time you would share more information with your employees?   0   1   2   3   4   5
4. Do you wish that your employees would get to the point when they are talking to you?   0   1   2   3   4   5
5. Do you believe that the grapevine exists because employees are too nosy?   0   1   2   3   4   5

Scoring

Total your scores for the five questions.

If your total score is from 18 to 25: You need to realize that you are not communicating with your employees. Take the initiative to be more open and straightforward with them. Treat them as you like to be treated by your supervisor.

If your total score is from 9 to 17: Your inconsistency may be interpreted as favoritism to others by those who feel left out at times. Share information with everyone equally and try to eliminate any tendency you might have to only half listen.

If your total score is from 0 to 8: Your workers probably feel in on things and confident about what they are supposed to do and about your willingness to listen to them. Continue the good communication skills that you are now practicing.

Supportive Work Relationships

Today's high-performance workplace requires a leader who understands the importance of a new work atmosphere. In such an atmosphere, workers can gain confidence in themselves and in one another and can develop supportive work relationships.

Every individual has the right to know what is expected of him or her and how his or her performance is being evaluated by others. Every individual must also have the right to ask questions and to seek clarification on any point, at any time.

The *freeing* leader creates conditions that encourage mutual respect mutual trust, and open communications. It is in such an environment that workers can help in the development of supportive work relationships, while, at the same time, each retains his or her individual identity.

Ultimately, if the human spirit is to be liberated in the workplace, the partnerships that reside in these supportive relationships will play a major role.

P A R T

III

THE APPROACH: EMPLOYEE-CENTERED LEADERSHIP

Leaders have faith in people. They believe that most people want to do a good job, and they see themselves as catalysts that help others accomplish that goal.

Chapter 7

The Critical Variable: Interdependence

In order for companies to survive into the new century, they will have to find leaders who rely less on their own accomplishments and more on the team approach—leaders who are less independent and more interdependent.

In an earlier day, the idea that people are the most important asset of an organization would have been scoffed at. However, in most successful companies today, the primary job of the leader is perceived as moving the organization towards its established goals by ensuring that the right people are hired, trained, and given the opportunity to do their job in an atmosphere that promotes creativity and effectiveness.

In this country, we have always admired the "rugged individualist." When we promote from within to fill supervisory and lower-level management jobs, we often choose the employee who has been tops in productivity. This may very well be the person who deserves the opportunity to advance. However, without adequate training, and without a clear understanding of the requirements of the new job, this person may find it difficult to rely on the performance of others while functioning in a supportive role.

Before I was promoted to supervisor, I ran a machine, and I didn't pay much attention to anyone else. I knew that some of the guys had problems with downtime, but it didn't impact me. As soon as I moved to supervision, reducing downtime became one of my responsibilities. The more I investigated the problem, the more it became apparent that I needed to get input from lots of other people, but asking others for help or suggestions was new to me.

After several months, the company sent me to a program on team building. I picked up several good ideas on how to involve employees in problem solving. I used these techniques, and, by working together, we made several improvements that reduced total downtime.

I'm getting better at working with others to solve problems, but I still have to overcome my old tendencies to 'go it alone.'

(Supervisor)

In his book, *The Seven Habits of Highly Effective People*, Stephen Covey describes people who have matured beyond independence and are becoming interdependent. The idea is that you cannot be interdependent until you have first been independent. Therefore, you are not independent or interdependent; you are either independent or independent *and* interdependent.

Think for a moment of people you would describe as "strong, rugged individualists." Now think of people you consider to be leaders. Most likely, everyone you thought of in each category is independent. However, the latter group, those you thought of as leaders, are also interdependent in their interactions with others.

There are at least three key factors that distinguish the independent person from the interdependent person. These factors are identified in the following table.

INDEPENDENCE	*INTERDEPENDENCE*
"I" focus	"We" focus
Trusts self	Trusts self and others
As I succeed, I am fulfilled	As others succeed, I am fulfilled

COMPARING AND CONTRASTING THE FACTORS

"I" focus versus "We" focus

Independent people are focused on themselves. They think in terms of "What can I do about this situation" and "How do I feel about this matter." They think in terms of individual decision making and see it as a personal challenge to figure out the answers.

On the other hand, interdependent people believe that "we" can do it better together than "I" can do it alone. They work with and through others to maximize results.

Obviously, it takes a "we" focused organization to empower its employees so that they feel a sense of responsibility and control over their jobs.

> My company has formed us into what they call, 'involvement teams.' Once I was on a team, I was trained on some basic quality tools, like flow charts and nominal group technique. I also got a crash course on team problem solving.
>
> Each team meets every week, on company time, to look at potential projects that would make things better in their own work area. Most of the time, we work on little things, but sometimes it's those kinds of things that drive you nuts.
>
> We have our own budget and have authorization to spend up to $1,500, without approval, on items that aren't directly tied to our product. When we have an idea that is tied to the product, we have to present the final recommendation to our supervisor.
>
> At first, some of the guys made fun of us, but now lots of those same guys have asked to get on a team. They want to be a part of this process too. What I like best about this whole approach is that we are actually making a difference, and our ideas are making this a better place to work.
>
> (Factory worker)

Most organizations today talk about their involvement in the quality movement and about their commitment to the concept of continuous improvement. Unless an organization has moved from an "I" focus to a "We" focus, their quality effort is either limited or theoretical since employee involvement is such an integral part of this commitment.

Trusts Self versus Trusts Self and Others

For the independent person, belief in self results from past successes that have led to feelings of self-confidence. If you are independent, you trust yourself more than you trust others. Why involve others when you know you will do it right and on time? Besides, there have been those times that you tried to rely on others, and sometimes they have let you down.

Delegation is difficult for the independent person. First of all, training usually precedes delegation. The independent person can rationalize that he or she can perform the task himself or herself in less time than the training would take, plus he or she would have the assurance that everything would be done correctly. Also, delegation includes some loss of control, and the independent person likes to stay in control.

> I used to get excited when my boss handed me a project and told me that it was 'my baby.' I soon found out that she really can't let go of even a small item. She always starts out checking on your progress, then she makes some suggestions on what you should do, and finally she decides to work with you, which really means that the whole project is on its way back to her office.
>
> At first, I thought she just lacked confidence in me, but then

I noticed that she does the same thing to everyone. Now we all realize it's her style—she just can't relinquish control.

(Industrial engineer)

For the interdependent person, trust does not stop with the self. It extends to others as well. Thus the interdependent person is perceived as enabling. He or she is not afraid to ask for or listen to others' opinions, and she or he views delegation as part of the process of freeing others.

As I Succeed, I Am Fulfilled versus As Others Succeed, I Am Fulfilled

For independent people, personal success leads to feelings of personal fulfillment. Within organizations they may be viewed by others as "heroes" or "star performers." Because of their apparently high level of self-confidence, you may be drawn to the independent person. While you may admire and respect the hero, you want to follow the person you view as a leader. Ford Motor Company recognizes the risk inherent in an organization filled with only independent people and has, according to Tom Peters, adopted the slogan, "No more heroes."

For the interdependent person, there is truly more of a feeling of fulfillment when success includes others. Developing others is a deep source of satisfaction.

Warren Bennis, in his book, *Leaders on Leadership* (Cambridge: Harvard Business Book, 1992), quotes Irwin Federman, president and CEO of Monolithic Memories, on this subject:

If you think about it, people love others not for who they are, but for how they make us feel. We willingly follow others for much the same reason. It makes us feel good to do so. Now, we also follow platoon sergeants, self-centered geniuses, demanding spouses, bosses of various persuasions, and others, for a variety of reasons as well. But none of these reasons involves the person's leadership qualities. In order to willingly accept the direction of another individual, it must feel good to do so. This business of making another person feel good in the unspectacular course of his daily comings and goings is, in my view, the very essence of leadership.

THE STEPS TO BECOMING MORE INTERDEPENDENT

Step 1: Become Convinced That a "We" Focus Is Better Than an "I" Focus

Until you become convinced that *freeing others* is superior to *controlling others*, you will not make a commitment to change. Once you are convinced, acting in a more interdependent manner will come fairly easily. The necessary sequence of events is *belief, commitment, action.*

Let me explain with a brief story. I have a friend who was a heavy smoker. He is married and has two young children. Whenever his smoking was discussed, he was very vocal that *his* smoking was *his* business and he would do what *he* wanted. He also admitted, at times, that quitting would be too difficult.

One day, he went to the doctor for something simple and as a result learned he had a tumor in his bladder. The doctor told him that his heavy smoking could be a contributing factor. That day, as he walked out of the doctor's office, he threw his pack of cigarettes away, and he has never touched another one since.

A significant emotional event made him a believer, and commitment and action quickly followed. (By the way, the tumor was removed with laser surgery, and he is doing well.)

Reading books such as, *The Seven Habits of Highly Effective People, The Fifth Discipline, Stewardship,* and *Leadership Is an Art* may certainly help you become convinced you should become more interdependent. All of these classics contain helpful examples of why a "we" focus is more effective than an "I" focus.

Seeking out and observing those who both believe in the freeing process and practice it daily will provide opportunities for you to see the passion with which many of these people practice the art of leadership. You will also see employees who are working as partners in the workplace and who have a refreshing outlook about work.

Step 2: Practice

No one has ever made the transition from being independent to interdependent as quickly as my friend went from smoker to nonsmoker. You will have to work very hard at allowing others to make suggestions and decisions and otherwise share in the day-to-day activities you formerly considered to be part of your private world of management.

When you slip back into old habits, you will have to recommit yourself to interdependence. Most of these slips will occur when the pressures of time and problems are the greatest. Eventually, it will become clear that this is when you need the input and support of others the most.

PEOPLE WORKING TOGETHER CAN DO ALMOST ANYTHING

Interdependent leaders recognize their responsibility to focus on their people rather than on themselves. Their efforts are to involve others. They use their position to develop win–win situations and to eliminate those that are win–lose. They view each one of their employees as an individual and tailor their approach with each so as to provide the greatest opportunity for job success and growth. They invite others to join them in mastering the challenges that will arise, and even more important, they help each one to reach beyond him- or herself and to accomplish things that he or she might have felt incapable of achieving.

Again quoting from Jim Hayes (*Memos for Management: LEADERSHIP,* New York: AMACON, 1983):

> An effective organization is a living thing: An organization is its people. People breathe life and purpose and energy into an organization. An organization has a manner, spirit, tempo, nature, character. It has moods, joys, fears, and sorrows. But most important of all, an organization has a purpose that is shared by all its members and to which they willingly commit their efforts. People working together can do almost anything.

People-centered leaders are both independent and interdependent. They recognize that it is the people within an organization that can make the difference, and they invite them on an adventure that has a much better chance of success if it's a joint effort.

Taking Stock

Instructions: For each statement, circle the number that most closely represents how often that statement is true for you. Use the following as a guide:

Almost never 0	Seldom 1	Occasionally 2	Frequently 3	Usually 4	Almost always 5

1. When faced with a complex task, is one of your first thoughts, "I can do this myself"? 0 1 2 3 4 5

2. Do you view delegation as a loss of control? 0 1 2 3 4 5

3. Do you feel a greater sense of satisfaction with a personal success than with one that involves the efforts of your employees? 0 1 2 3 4 5

4. Do you believe that for you to "win," someone else must "lose"? 0 1 2 3 4 5

5. Do you believe that people working together usually cause unnecessary problems? 0 1 2 3 4 5

Scoring

Total your scores for the five questions.

If your total score is from 18 to 25: Your workers probably feel cheated, as far as training is concerned, and more than likely view you as a "control freak." You need to develop a "we" approach.

If your total score is from 9 to 17: Your workers are probably very frustrated. Your actions "tease" them: Sometimes you give them responsibility; other times you don't. Once they have experienced some sense of ownership, it is even harder on them when you take it back. Reflect on the times you have involved them and the reactions you got. Concentrate on involving others.

If your total score is from 0 to 8: Your workers probably feel you value their opinions and their efforts, and they normally seek greater responsibilities with confidence. Keep up the good work and continue to prepare your best employees for promotion.

Chapter 8

Dealing with the Disruptive Employee

There might be some who would initially have difficulty making this chapter "fit" with those that preceded it. However, I believe that there is more consistency in what I am suggesting than may be apparent at first glance.

Up until now, I have emphasized the need for the leader to *free*, rather than to *control* employees. This chapter features a situation that requires control: the presence of a disruptive employee.

Regardless of your best efforts to create a motivating environment, there is a chance you may have at least one employee who will not respond. Since motivation comes from within, it isn't surprising that in any work group there could be someone who isn't motivated by work or the characteristics of a motivating environment.

There is nothing wrong with your trying to influence such an individual to change. However, it is important to understand that if your best efforts fail, this doesn't mean you are a failure. During my career, I have seen managers and supervisors accept the blame for the negative actions of employees who would not have responded positively to anyone in authority.

THE IMPORTANCE OF CORRECTIVE ACTION

When you have an employee who acts in a disruptive way, it is imperative that you take the necessary steps to correct the situation. If you do not, the morale of your good workers will suffer, and they will lose respect for you as the leader.

Since we were closed for inventory, I scheduled a meeting with the sales clerks to discuss some product changes that would be occurring in about a month. There were two department employees who had no direct sales contacts or responsibilities. I explained to them that the meeting was about sales, so they could work on the inventory instead of attending.

Just as I started the meeting, in walked the two employees. I stopped and asked them if they needed something. One of them, named Jane, spoke up. 'We decided that we should be in on a department meeting like this.' I answered, 'As I told you earlier, I don't think that it is necessary for you to attend since you don't work in sales, so I would appreciate it if you would go back to working on the inventory.'

Kay, the other employee, started to make a move for the door, but Jane stood her ground. She spoke up again, 'I would rather stay and hear what you are talking about to the other department employees.'

I realized that Jane was trying to turn this little incident into a showdown, so I decided that I needed to respond in a like manner. I said, 'Jane, I don't think that you need to be in on this meeting, so you have two choices at this point: One is to go back to work, and the other is to go home. It's your decision, but you will have to decide quickly, because I want to get this meeting started.'

Jane glared at me and then followed Kay, who was already going out the door.

After the meeting, one of the other employees gave me a big smile and a 'thumbs up' sign as she left the room. Later, several employees told me they were glad that someone finally stood up to Jane, since she always was looking for ways to cause some type of problem.

(Store buyer)

Look at how one worker responded to a newspaper article that had indicated that employers respond positively to good employees and take the appropriate action against disruptive employees.

Dear Gentlemen:

Employers do not always respect and value good employees, so I disagree with what you said in a recent column. You noted, 'Most bosses probably feel more positive toward employees who are capable, resourceful, and winning at work. They cause you no problems. In contrast, losers make work a nightmare.'

Well, this does not hold true in my job. We have a few employees who are incompetent. Management just lets them get away with it. It's incredible.

Where I work, there are several employees who are conscientious, hard-working self-starters, but they're browbeaten and used as scapegoats for both their own and these others' errors.

How do you explain this? It defies all logic. I've seen this a lot throughout my long career. You can't tell me employers respect and place a high value on good employees. I've seen too much of the other—the good ones receiving little credit, and the lousy ones being given all sorts of accolades.

You are not all that realistic. I've had a lot of experience and know what I'm talking about.

Disagreeing

THE NEED FOR CONSEQUENCES RELATED TO ACTIONS

There are entire organizations that seem to operate without there being any real consequences for the good and bad things that happen. Author Judith Bardwick writes about the conditions that can lead to that type of atmosphere in her book, *Danger in the Comfort Zone.*[1]

> In organizations where there is no sense of urgency, morale and motivation are usually very low. There's no vitality, no energy. And what of the people who work in those organizations? At first, such total security seems wonderful. But before long, a kind of heavy complacency settles in. When the system is unresponsive, when the organization does not require work that makes a difference, when outstanding performers are not rewarded for their accomplishments, and when underachieving performers are not punished, people become apathetic. In organizations where nothing much happens regardless of whether you do something exceptional or just show up in the morning, the people lose heart and motivation is reduced near the lowest common denominator.

Establishing consequences for actions and then consistently ensuring that an action results in an appropriate positive or negative consequence is one of the keys to developing credibility with your people. A disruptive employee quickly learns whether it matters or not if he or she responds to rules and regulations and whether there are consequences for unacceptable behavior in the workplace.

CORRECTING THE DISRUPTIVE EMPLOYEE

If you are in a leadership role and have an employee who will not respond to your best efforts, and you see a need for change, try the following four steps:

---

[1] Reprinted, with permission of the publisher, from DANGER IN THE COMFORT ZONE by Judith M. Bardwick, © 1995 Judith M. Bardwick, Ph.D., Inc. Published by AMACOM, a division of the American Management Association. All rights reserved.

Step 1: Be Proud of Yourself for Facing Up to the Problem

Some managers and supervisors avoid confrontation and look the other way when an employee breaks rules or otherwise disrupts the workplace. Some of these people have little signs on their desks that say things like "The Buck Stops Here." Many have hypertension or other symptoms of job stress, and some talk about being burned out.

So be proud of yourself. You know you have a problem, and you have decided to do something about it. At the same time, realize that it may take real resolve on your part to change the existing situation.

Step 2: Decide What Changes Are Needed

Think about the changes that are needed within your area of responsibility. Concentrate on the major items that affect the greatest number of people and cause the most disruption. Picture in your mind the conditions that would exist if each of these items were changed to your satisfaction. Once you know what must be changed, develop a series of action steps that will make the changes happen.

Step 3: Have a Heart-to-Heart Talk with Your Disruptive Employee

This step marks the point of no return. Once you have this discussion, there is no turning back. If you don't go forward, your credibility will be so damaged it will be irreparable.

This is not a time to mince words with this employee. The manner in which you handle this meeting will help set the tone for the future. In a straightforward manner, tell the individual what you believe is right and wrong with the present environment. There is nothing wrong with admitting that your approach has contributed to the problem. Also, there is nothing wrong with allowing your employee to have his or her say, but don't allow matters to get out of hand.

Next, tell the employee how things are going to be different in the future. If you plan on handling certain matters differently, tell the employee what the "new you" plans to do. This part of the discussion doesn't lend itself to much input from the employee although you may want to answer questions or clarify any matters that he or she doesn't feel are clear. End by stating exactly when the new ways of doing things will begin. You may want to give the employee until the next morning to think about what you have said, but don't wait too long since the changes are needed.

Step 4: Walk the Talk

Start when you said you would start and do what you said you would do. Chances are that you will be tested early on. If you are, you must take the necessary action to reinforce your outlined plan and to emphasize that you will be dealing with the employee in terms of consequences from now on.

THE STORY OF SCOTT

The use of these steps can best be illustrated by telling the story of Scott, who saved his job and, more importantly, his health and well-being by getting in control in a tough situation.

Scott had been in a supervisory job for about five years when I met him. His job was one that I would classify as high stress. He dealt continuously with the production-control people who represented all of the major automobile firms in this country. He also supervised five other people in a department of a company that was a major supplier to the automotive industry.

His department handled the production-control function for his firm. It received the orders from the automotive companies, scheduled these orders through the production process, and placed priorities on the shipping department to ensure timely packaging and shipping.

A late shipment could result in a production line's being shut down in an automotive plant, and the cost of such a shutdown could be charged back against the supplier. Therefore, Scott always seemed to be dealing with one crisis after another.

The first time I visited Scott on the job, I was struck by two things. First, he looked and acted like he might have a heart attack or a stroke at any minute, while, at the same time, his employees seemed relaxed and almost uninvolved in what was going on around them. Scott's face was beet red, and he had big red blotches on his neck that looked like hives. His phone rang constantly, and several times he told a caller that he would check on their shipment and call them back. On two occasions, employees transferred calls to Scott.

Needless to say, we visited very little, and I left filled with concern.

About a week later, I had the chance to talk to Scott after an evening meeting of a civic group. He started out by apologizing for the chaos that made a visit at his work impossible. He then moved into some remarks about how badly things were going at work.

"You know," he said, "sometimes, I don't know who I'm the most upset with: our customers, who want everything yesterday; my employees, who won't get involved; or myself, for letting things get this way."

We talked for a long time that evening. I mostly listened as Scott shared his frustrations and wondered out loud about how much longer he could put up with things as they were.

After a while, I asked him to tell me how things ought to be rather than how they actually were. I said, "Tell me what you would like things to be like and what would have to be done to get things to that point."

With only minor hesitations, he was able to outline a system that would place the responsibility for a different customer on each of his employees. "That would make it possible for me to act as the overall supervisor and to deal only with the exceptions," he said.

The longer we talked, the more excited he got. Finally, I asked him, "Why don't you implement a system like the one you just described?"

He got very quiet for a few minutes, and then he said, "I have allowed the people who work for me to get to the point that they delegate to me, instead of the other way around. They have gotten lazy, and I have allowed it to happen. When things get tough, they just give the problem to me and forget about it."

There was another long pause, and then Scott spoke again. "I have to put things back like they should be, or I'm not going to last. I can't let things go on like they are now."

Before we parted company that evening, Scott had talked through who would be assigned to each customer, how the calls would be handled in the future, and how he would explain the new duties to each of his employees. I asked him if he was ready to deal with the first time one of his employees tried to give him his or her work. He said, "I'd better be or nothing will change, and things are going to have to change."

Later, Scott told me he'd met with his employees and told them of the changes. He said the meeting got a little testy at times and that he had to give one employee an ultimatum but that he did implement the revised system, and things were going much better. He said that, at first, there were several attempts to get him to handle situations as he would have done previously but that he stood firm and told the employees to go ahead without his direct involvement.

I had the occasion to visit Scott at work about four months later. The entire atmosphere was different, and Scott no longer looked like a candidate for a cardiac ward. There was still lots of pressure, but there seemed to be a team dealing with the challenges of the day.

THE VALUE IN CORRECTING A BAD SITUATION

Dealing directly with a problem employee may be difficult and taxing. However, failure to do so will not make the situation go away. In fact, trying to ignore a disruptive employee will usually lead to a more disruptive situation.

Remember, the people who will most appreciate your efforts to correct a bad situation will be your good employees.

Taking Stock

Instructions: For each statement, circle the number that most closely represents how often that statement is true for you. Use the following as a guide:

Almost never 0	Seldom 1	Occasionally 2	Frequently 3	Usually 4	Almost always 5

1. If you have a disruptive employee, do you hope the situation will correct itself?   0 1 2 3 4 5

2. Do you ignore an employee who breaks rules?   0 1 2 3 4 5

3. If an employee challenged a directive in front of other employees, would you ignore his or her comments?   0 1 2 3 4 5

4. Do you find it difficult to apply a negative consequence to a negative action?   0 1 2 3 4 5

5. Do you establish limits and then back down if an employee goes beyond them?   0 1 2 3 4 5

Scoring

Total your scores for the five questions.

If your total score is from 18 to 25: Your work area is probably in turmoil. Your good workers are upset because you don't take the necessary steps to eliminate disruptive situations. As hard as it might be, you must take immediate and direct action to regain control.

If your total score is from 9 to 17: Your good workers are probably unhappy with you. They view you as inconsistent and unwilling to tackle the tough issues. You must confront every situation in a consistent manner and build an image as someone who is fair but tough when necessary.

If your total score is from 0 to 8: Everyone that works for you may not like you, but they respect you. They know you are consistent and fair and that you will take on a difficult situation without hesitation. Keep up the good work!

Chapter 9

Building Corporate Community

In the past, organizational structure has encouraged empire building and turf-protection practices. Today, the employee-centered leader is helping to create a new type of work environment. Author James Autry speaks of such an environment in his book, *Love and Profit* (New York: Avon Books, 1992).

> So we managers have the opportunity to lead and direct people in that ever more powerful bond of common enterprise, and at the same time to create a place of friendship, deep personal connections, and neighborhood. So how about this for a new management bumper sticker: IF YOU'RE NOT CREATING COMMUNITY, YOU'RE NOT MANAGING.

Considering the amount of time that each of us spends on the job and the number of times we must count on one another if we are to succeed, it seems that the work environment would function as a place of friendship, rather than a center for distrust.

This has not been the case, however, because historically businesses have operated with a "win–lose" approach: For my business to succeed, yours must fail; for me to get ahead, you must be pushed aside.

A NEW WAY OF OPERATING: EVERYBODY WINS

Today, there is a new approach, called "win–win". As the name implies, this approach is based on the concept that there doesn't have to be a loser for every winner. Win–win says that if we work together, we can all win.

Much of what is happening today with cross-functional work teams and self-directed work teams is the result of this philosophy. Many companies have retired their old organizational charts. These firms have moved away from a structure rooted in the trappings of vertical silos, with each silo representing a traditional functional area of business such as accounting, production, or sales. They have found that, by breaking with tradition, they can organize across those silos and bring people together who previously knew little about each other's problems or needs. Dynamic, interrelated teams are now tackling problems together in a spirit of interdependence and cooperation that was previously nonexistent.

> I am part of a new team that is working on ways to reduce the downtime that we have because our security records storage area is so far away from our work area. It sounded like a simple problem when we started, but we have people from three different areas working on it and we still haven't come up with the right answer. One thing though, we all appreciate each other's problems more.
>
> (Receptionist)

> We used to operate in a hostile environment. The company didn't trust us and we didn't trust them. When they first came to us and said that they wanted to start over and asked us what was on our minds, we just laughed. We figured it was just another trick of some kind.
>
> It took a long time, but things really are better. Now we can make suggestions, and if a supervisor asks us to do something, we can say something like, 'Have you ever thought of trying it this way?'
>
> I think the company has gained, and most of us feel like what we are doing does make a difference.
>
> (Factory worker)

It used to be that if I made a suggestion about any of the com-
puter programs, I would be ignored, or someone would put
me down.

Today, the company asks for our suggestions, and they
have a new slogan that is posted everywhere. It says, 'They
aren't *my* problems or *your* problems, they are *our* problems—
LET'S WORK TOGETHER TO SOLVE THEM.'

There are a couple of changes that I suggested that have
been written up in the company newsletter. It makes you try
to think of other improvements.

(Data entry clerk)

Organizations like these have come to the realization
that there are enough dragons to slay outside of the company. They have tried to eliminate the internal bloodletting
that is encouraged when there is competition between employees. These companies are encouraging employees to
bring the same skills and approaches to the workplace that
they practice in the other areas of their lives.

In such an atmosphere, each individual can be recognized and accepted as just that, an individual, with gifts
that are meant to be shared with others.

THE ELEMENTS OF COMMUNITY

It is in such a setting that the elements essential to the development of community can flourish. These elements are
stability, interdependence, unity, and trust.

Stability

For the members of an organization to consider it a form of
community, they have to have confidence that certain aspects of the organization will not change. This confidence
cannot be entirely rooted in individuals because individu-

als will come and go, if for no other reason than retirement.

The reasons the organization exists can provide part of the necessary foundation for stability if they are carefully determined and clearly stated in a mission statement that is reflected in the organization's method of operating.

An example of one company's effort to provide its employees with a clear statement of its operating beliefs is presented by author Richard M. Hodgetts in his AMA management briefing, "Blueprints for Continuous Improvement." He states that AT&T Universal Card Services gives each employee a card that describes the organization's philosophy and goals.

Customer delight. We delight our customers by exceeding their expectations.

Teamwork. Teams make things happen when everybody's voice is heard.

Mutual respect. Each of us deserves to be treated with dignity.

Commitment. UCS people will meet and deliver what they promise to each other and to our customers.

Continuous improvement. Each day, we should seek to get a little bit better since small improvements, added up, bring us closer to our goals.

Sense of urgency. We will move quickly to accomplish our goals, meet our commitments, and delight our customers.

Trust and integrity. We will trust one another to accomplish what we say we will accomplish. We will conduct ourselves— in dealing with customers and colleagues—with integrity always.

Interdependence

Interdependence is a necessary element of any community because all the members must be able to count on one another. In fact, each member must be able to demand all that another can give and, at the same time, be willing to give all that she or he is able to give when asked.

As Stephen Covey says in, *The Seven Habits of Highly Effective People* (New York: Simon & Schuster Trade, 1990):

> Interdependence opens up worlds of possibilities for deep, rich, meaningful associations, for geometrically increased productivity, for serving, for contributing, for learning, for growing.

Interdependence is one of the key factors in the development of self-directed work groups within an organization. As interdependence grows, employees see themselves as part of a group rather than as individuals who operate independently. Each employee contributes from his or her areas of strength, and everyone feels free to solicit the help of others when it's needed.

Traditional organizational structure cannot be allowed to interfere in this process. To the contrary, if the structure is interfering with the organization's level of interdependence, this is a clear sign that the structure is in need of modification.

Unity

Unity in the workplace is the result of people having a common aim. A unified organizational aim is possible if the following steps are taken:

1. A clear mission statement is developed and then periodically reviewed and refined, as necessary.

2. This mission statement is communicated to all of the employees within the organization and their commitment to its ideals is fervently solicited.

Each member of an organization must be encouraged to be a self-starter and to practice self-discipline. At the same time, each must be asked to integrate his or her personal goals with those of the organization. Employees who are able to work for the common good are capable of fostering workplace unity. Breaking down the barriers that separate employees and encouraging everyone to utilize his or her individual gifts for the betterment of the whole, is the key to building unity.

Trust

If trust prevails, individuals are free to enter into their work relationships in an open manner, with the confidence that they will be accepted as they are and that the vulnerabilities that they expose will not be used against them in a harmful way. In an atmosphere of trust, employees will offer suggestions and will generally be willing to risk more in all of their work situations.

> If businesses are to thrive in the global marketplace, trust must be more than something that is talked about; it must be at the core of everything that is done. Organizations cannot be jungles where only the fittest survive, living in a state of battle readiness in order to meet the grueling tests of everyday corporate life. If companies are to motivate employees and win their loyalty, they must change the way relationships are constructed.
>
> Frank K. Sonnenberg
> *Managing with a Conscience*
> (New York: McGraw-Hill, 1992)

THE LEADER AS FACILITATOR OF COMMUNITY

Much is being written today on the subject of leadership that places the leader in a new role: as servant or steward.

As such, the leader can function as the facilitator of a work-place community.

> Instead of deciding what kind of culture to create, and thus defining purpose, stewards can ask that each member of the organization decide what the place will become. Stewardship also asks us to forsake caretaking, an even harder habit to give up. We do not serve other adults when we take responsibility for their well-being. We continue to care, but when we care-take, we treat others, especially those in low power positions, as if they were not able to provide for themselves.
>
> Peter Block
> *Stewardship*
> (San Francisco: Berrett-Koehler Pub, 1993)

> The difference manifests itself in the care taken by the servant—first to make sure that other people's highest priority needs are being served. The best test, and difficult to administer, is: Do those served grow as persons? Do they, while being served, become healthier, wiser, freer, more autonomous, more likely themselves to become servants? And, what is the effect on the least privileged in society; will they benefit, or, at least not be further deprived?
>
> Robert K. Greenleaf
> *Servant Leadership*
> (New Jersey: Paulist Pr., 1977)

As the facilitator of community, the leader trains employees to perform many of the functions and responsibilities that traditionally have been performed by a supervisor or manager. For example, the employees are often delegated the responsibility for making the final hiring decision on new hires that will be working with them.

The leader releases responsibilities to the employees, as they are trained and become capable of handling them. The leader eventually evolves into a facilitator or advisor, who clarifies expectations, removes roadblocks, and is otherwise available to the employees on an as-needed basis.

CONFLICTS WILL STILL EXIST

Just because employees are working together does not mean that conflicts will be entirely eliminated. On the contrary, there may be a more open exchange of ideas and opinions than there were when employees were urged to conform and to follow mandates from above. In this new setting, employees need to be encouraged to surface conflicts rather than suppress them. At the same time, they should be trained to resolve conflicts through open, two-way discussion that includes two-way listening and compromise whenever it is appropriate.

Roger D'Aprix speaks of such an environment in his book, *Struggle for Identity* (Chicago: Dow-Jones, Irwin, 1972).

> The critical task for corporate management in the months and years ahead will be to respond to this new requirement for individual fulfillment, to redirect their efforts in establishing an environment where this kind of self-discovery is not only possible, but where it is encouraged, even required. To establish an environment where people can admit conflict openly and confront one another without distrust and intolerance, where disagreement is not considered threatening—in short, where there is a community of self-enlightened and tolerant people working for goals they understand and generally share.

Employees in a workforce that is able to attain this level of activity will develop a high degree of empathy for one another and will develop a level of commitment to one another.

THE NEED FOR A REORDERING OF PRIORITIES

If it is impossible to integrate an organization's goals with the development of those who work there, a reordering of priorities is needed.

In an organization that is trying to create community, there needs to be a new atmosphere, a new approach—a caring approach—which encourages the development of new bonds in the workplace.

TAKING STOCK

Instructions: For each statement, circle the number that most closely represents how often that statement is true for you. Use the following as a guide:

Almost never 0	Seldom 1	Occasionally 2	Frequently 3	Usually 4	Almost always 5

1. Do you encourage win–lose solutions?   0 1 2 3 4 5
2. Are you suspicious of cross-functional work teams because of possible loss of personal control?   0 1 2 3 4 5
3. Do you believe you should retain all authority and responsibility to ensure proper accountability?   0 1 2 3 4 5
4. Do you encourage your employees to compete with one another?   0 1 2 3 4 5
5. Do you believe that the concept of community does not belong in the workplace?   0 1 2 3 4 5

Scoring

Total your scores for the five questions.

If your total score is from 18 to 25: Your work area probably features competition rather than cooperation. As a result, your workers may withhold information from one another in an effort to gain an advantage. Be open and trusting and encourage the same type of approach from your workers.

If your total score is from 9 to 17: Because of the mixed signals you send, your workers probably don't take chances on opening up to others. Your workplace may be filled with suspicion and doubt. If more of your decisions encourage a win–win approach, your workers will cooperate with one another more.

If your total score is from 0 to 8: Your workers are probably congenial and helpful to one another, and they approach you with ideas and suggestions of ways to improve things. Continue to encourage a friendly and communitylike atmosphere.

A Win-Win Approach

Employee-centered leadership is based on trust and is deeply rooted in the actions of the interdependent leader. It is an approach that can produce positive effects for everyone concerned.

Employees in such an environment are given the freedom to develop and grow. They share in the creative approaches that are developed and therefore more clearly understand the importance of the roles they assume.

Those who are not willing to be part of the solution are viewed as part of the problem, and their inappropriate actions are dealt with in terms of properly ordered consequences. This is done because it is the fair thing to do for them as well as for those who are working together to eliminate obstacles.

Employee-centered leaders welcome this new approach, which allows them to serve as facilitators rather than control artists. Each understands that when she or he is doing her or his job, others will feel they are functioning on their own, with little or no assistance from the leader.

It is in such an atmosphere that a work-based community can develop—a community of individuals who will work collectively for the betterment of the whole and who will accomplish their tasks while respecting and nurturing one another.

IV

THE COMMITMENT: TO ACCEPT THE RESPONSIBILITIES OF LEADERSHIP

We live in a fast-paced, ever-changing world that is going to demand much from its future leaders. Those who are successful will have an operating philosophy that anchors their actions as they blend the needs of the organization and those of the workforce into a win–win combination.

Chapter 10

Developing Your Operating Philosophy

Do you remember how Charles Dickens described Ebenezer Scrooge's leadership style?

> Oh! but he was a tight-fisted hand at the grindstone, Scrooge! A squeezing, scraping, clutching, covetous old sinner! Hard and sharp as flint, from which no steel had ever struck out generous fire, secret, and self-contained, and solitary as an oyster. . . .
>
> He carried his own low temperature always about with him; he iced his office in the dog-days; and didn't thaw it one degree at Christmas. . . .
>
> The door of Scrooge's counting-house was open, that he might keep his eye upon his clerk, who, in a dismal little cell beyond, a sort of tank, was copying letters. Scrooge had a very small fire, but the clerk's fire was so very much smaller that it looked like one coal. But he couldn't replenish it, for Scrooge kept the coal-box in his own room, and so surely as the clerk came in with the shovel, the master predicted that it would be necessary for them to part. . . .

Very few, if any, managers would describe themselves as harshly as Dickens described Ebenezer Scrooge. Of course, prior to the visits from the spirits, Scrooge saw nothing wrong with his way of dealing with others, and he certainly would have disagreed with Dickens's evaluation.

It was during the visit from the ghost of Christmas yet to come that Scrooge verbalized the need for a change of heart and a change in his way of doing things:

The finger pointed from the grave to him, and back again.
'No, Spirit! Oh, no, no!'
The finger still was there.
'Spirit!' he cried, tight clutching at its robe, 'hear me! I am not the man I was. I will not be the man I must have been but for this intercourse.'

As the story ends, it depicts a changed Ebenezer Scrooge.

"A merrier Christmas, Bob, my good fellow, than I have given you for many a year! I'll raise your salary, and endeavor to assist your struggling family, and we will discuss your affairs this very afternoon, over a Christmas bowl of smoking bishop, Bob! Make up the fires, and buy another coal-shuttle before you dot another i, Bob Cratchit!"
Scrooge was better than his word. He did it all, and infinitely more; and to Tiny Tim, who did not die, he was a second father. He became as good a friend, as good a master, and as good a man as the good old City knew, or any other good old city, town, or borough in the good old world."

A VISIT WITH YOUR OWN SPIRITS

You might think that no one has ever had an experience like old Scrooge, but many have. Scrooge's series of visits from the spirits is very similar to what many people experience when they have a brush with death.

Talk to someone who has experienced a severe heart attack or who has battled a life-threatening illness such as cancer. Most will tell you that, at some time during their ordeal, they mentally had a visit with their own spirits from the past and present and that they thought about the fragile future and how differently they might approach it if they would only be given that opportunity.

After the second biopsy, the doctor's office called and said that he would like to see my wife and me on the following day. I knew it must be bad news when he said he wanted both of us to come in, but it still hit me hard when he said I had cancer. I had some choices, but when he said he believed it was operable, I told him to get the surgery scheduled.

As it ended up, I had two weeks to wait. Believe me, that was a long two weeks. Along the way, the doctor made it clear that if they found more than they suspected, they would not operate.

At the time, I was 45 years old and we had two children in college, one in high school, and one in grade school. I spent a lot of time thinking about what I might miss of their growing up, and I worried a lot about money.

I told the people at work that I would be back, at least part-time, within three months. Secretly, I wondered if I would ever be back.

I thought about some things that I would do differently, if everything turned out OK. I'm sure everyone in a similar position goes through the same thing.

To make a long story a little shorter, the cancer was operable and all the follow-up tests they have done have been negative, and it's been over 10 years now.

Did I change? In some ways, I did. First of all, I know I cherished every moment of my kids' growing up. I never took any of their childhood things for granted again.

At work, I'm not sure the changes were as long lasting. At first, some things didn't get to me as much as they did before, but after a while, I think I slipped back. One thing that did change though, I didn't let work interfere with family things anymore. Sometimes, I went back to work after a game or some school activity, but I didn't miss those kinds of events.

One other thing: I used to crab and complain every winter, from November until March. You know, I really mellowed out after the operation. I just appreciate being around to experience whatever kind of weather comes along.

(Labor attorney)

Given another chance, many people do change and look at life, and people, and life's situations in a different way. Others will tell you that they were somehow different for some period of time, but that, after a while, they reverted to their old selves. Of course, there are other events that will cause a person to pull up short and do some real soul-searching and self-evaluation. There are many who have lost their jobs in midlife and can thus identify with what I am saying.

THE NEED FOR A PERSONAL OPERATING PHILOSOPHY

Without something happening to jolt you out of your own little world, chances are you won't believe there is a need for you to do an honest self-appraisal and to take the steps necessary to make changes in your life.

However, leaders need to develop a personal operating philosophy. They need to articulate their beliefs and then measure what they do against what they believe to see if there is an acceptable level of consistency.

Leaders who take the time to write down their business credo are in a position to analyze how it applies to the way they manage themselves and others. In preparing such a personal philosophy, questions such as these need to be answered:

- What are the essential attributes of leadership, and what does each one mean to me?
- What is my potential?
- Am I making full use of my potential?
- What are my responsibilities to my company?
- What are my responsibilities to those who report to me?
- What am I doing to continue to grow?
- How do I integrate my business and personal life?
- How do I help others integrate their business and personal lives?
- Can I be counted on when the going gets tough?
- What responsibility do I have to my community?

- Am I meeting my community responsibilities?
- What do I want to accomplish during the remainder of my work career?
- Does my present job situation provide the promise of self-actualization?
- Would I be willing to make a career move to avoid compromising my moral principles?

Writing down your beliefs can be time-consuming and difficult, but, once you have done it, you will refer to it often because the document will have real meaning to you.

DOCUMENTING YOUR BELIEFS IS JUST ONE OF MANY STEPS

In September 1985, an article written by Paul G. Engel appeared in *Industry Week* (September 16, 1985 p. 29–30) magazine. The article was entitled, "Are You Getting Stale?" and in it Mr. Engel says:

> You know the feeling. It's an unsettling, I-can't-quite-put-my-finger-on-it-unease—a sense that if you're not already peering over the edge into a professional black abyss, you're getting dangerously close. It can be a physical, as well as a mental, malady.
> Like a five-day-old slice of pumpernickel, you're stale.
> If the sense of staleness persists, it's probably your job—or your attitude toward the job—that's causing it. And don't think your age is a buffer if you're on the shy side of 40; it can happen to anyone.

Mr. Engel then discusses a list of "staleness" warning signs that he credits to consultants William Morin and Andrew Sherwood:

- Do you seem to be losing your corporate voice? Have co-workers, subordinates, and your bosses stopped communicating with you?

- Do you frequently resist change?
- Do you ignore the ideas and efforts of others?
- Are you getting negative feedback, perhaps as the result of negative thinking? ("It can't be done. It won't work.")
- Has your personal productivity been slipping?
- Are you missing assignment deadlines?
- Have you neglected to appraise your work and attitude on a regular basis?
- Do you measure results simply on the basis of personal gain?

William Morin and Andrew Sherwood then suggest that the more often you answer yes to these questions, the greater the probability that you're getting stale.

If you believe you're getting stale, Morin offers some advice. Briefly, he suggests the following:

1. **Don't panic.** "Congratulate yourself for being realistic and objective about your situation."
2. **Upgrade your resume.** "Not because you may be needing it soon, but because the process is a therapeutic step that helps you to begin to take stock of yourself."
3. **Consider your current job by putting together an informal job description.** "Try to decide what is good and bad about it. You'll see what you should be doing and, by extension, you'll learn whether you're actually performing these tasks."
4. **Draw up one additional document.** "Use an old-fashioned phrase and call it your *career-path statement*. Write down as much as you can about what you would like to be doing at this point in your career. Be specific. Don't shy away from mentioning how much money you would like to make or where you would be most happy living."

William Morin suggests that these documents allow you to look at yourself, "in the past, the present and the future."

The article ends with a quote from Andrew Sherwood: "You must continue to grow with the job in order to keep it and move up. There is no status quo in career advancement. Either you are moving forward—or you're slipping."

Answering the questions contained in this article and following the steps listed above, will help you to honestly evaluate whether staleness is an issue that you must confront as part of your self-assessment.

SELF-ASSESSMENT ALONE WON'T SUPPLY ALL THE ANSWERS

Self-assessment represents just one of the pieces needed to solve the leadership puzzle. It won't give you the complete answer.

As Max DePree says in *Leadership Is an Art* (New York: Doubleday, 1989):

> Leadership is much more an art, a belief, a condition of the heart, than a set of things to do. The visible signs of artful leadership are expressed, ultimately, in its practice.

However, once you have done this type of self-assessment, you may be aware of a new clarity in your approach as you practice the art of leadership.

THE NEED FOR FEEDBACK FROM OTHERS

Executives create environments that either encourage or discourage meaningful feedback about what is happening within the company and about how others view their performance. The things they do to create these environments may be done consciously or unconsciously.

> Even though I'm in a senior executive position, I still need feedback on how I do my job. I'm talking about the straight scoop on how I handle my relationships, my leadership style, my strengths and weaknesses, and those sorts of things. I've found that the higher your position, the harder it is to get honest feedback.
>
> (Senior vice president)

> Whenever we are in a meeting with the CEO, and he asks for feedback or opinions, there are signals that we watch for. If his face gets red, it's time to watch what you are saying. If he begins to interrupt a lot, it's best to not say much more. If he begins to use four letter-words, especially the "f" word, get ready to be ripped.
>
> (Vice president)

WAYS THAT FEEDBACK IS DISCOURAGED

The Abrasive Executive

This type of person takes advantage of his or her position to bully and intimidate others. His or her insensitivity to the feelings of others makes honest, two-way communication impossible.

> Sometimes our plant manager would stop by the lunchroom and visit with some of the employees while they were on break. This one day, the manager of engineering happened to be in there at the same time. I don't know exactly what happened, but all of a sudden, I was aware that it got real quiet, real quick.
>
> The plant manager was obviously chewing out the manager of engineering right there in the lunchroom, and right in front of about 25 hourly employees. He said some pretty nasty

things about his not meeting a deadline that cost the company a chance at a contract.

At one point, the manager of engineering started to say something, and the plant manager told him to 'shut up and just listen.'

People started getting up and quietly leaving. Pretty soon, only the two of them were left in the room. Those of us who were in there when it started were pretty embarrassed, and we felt sorry for the manager of engineering.

From then on, I got out of there whenever the plant manager came in. I figured if that could happen to one of the bosses, it sure as hell could happen to me.

(Warehouse worker)

Sometime later, I had the opportunity to talk to that manager of engineering about what had happened. The incident left him angry, embarrassed, and resentful. He told me that he felt his boss had taken advantage of his position and had shown that he was pretty much of a jerk to do something like that in a public place and in front of other people, especially hourly workers. He also told me that from that time on, whenever he was around the plant manager, he only spoke when it was absolutely necessary.

Obviously, the plant manager in this story needs a lot of help with his methods of dealing with others, but it's a good bet that none of his employees will volunteer that type of information. Even if he wanted feedback, which seems doubtful, it would be nearly impossible to create the conditions that would provide the needed level of anonymity for those providing the information.

Executive Exemption from Appraisal

Executives often feel they have the authority to declare themselves exempt from any type of appraisal. After all, who within the organization is going to argue with them?

I have been appraised and evaluated ever since I started my working career. Now that I've reached this level, I don't plan to sit through any more of those sessions. I've paid my dues. Now it's time for others to worry about what I think about their performance and to make the necessary changes that please me.

(Department manager)

Chances are good that an appraisal of this type of person would be meaningless anyway, but exclusion unfortunately ensures that no information will flow upward.

Time Away from the Workplace

If you aren't at work, it's easier to avoid involvement and feedback. Rather than "managing by walking around," some people "manage by traveling around." They find many excuses for staying *out* of touch. One time it's a seminar they need to attend in order to "stay current." Another time, it's the need to visit a supplier to make sure they are "staying on top of things." There's never a shortage of needs that require them to be away.

Our boss was complaining to several of us that he was going to have to be out of the office for the last two days of the next week. He said that he was especially upset since he had just been on a business trip that took him away for three days a few weeks earlier.

After he left, one of the guys told us that the last trip had been to the Masters, courtesy of one of our suppliers and that this time he was going to the Kentucky Derby.

(Middle manager)

Building a Staff of Cheerleaders

As was discussed in an earlier chapter, there are executives who reward staff members for presenting only the "good news" about the organization and for the ability to unwaveringly agree with whatever the executive says. Such executives can be assured of having a great group of cheerleaders who will only tell them what they want to hear and who will react positively to every idea the executives utter.

WAYS THAT FEEDBACK IS ENCOURAGED

Using a Third Party

I hired a consultant who had done some work for a friend of mine who also owns his own business. I told him that I wanted to find out how the people who worked for me felt about my leadership style and the way I made decisions. The report I got back was really helpful.

My people said that they admired and respected me. They also said that there were times that I overmanaged. They suggested that I allow trained employees a little more freedom in on-the-job decision making.

The consultant stressed that several of the people were hesitant to say anything that could be construed as negative because they didn't want me to think they were unappreciative or trying to complain.

The consultant was able to share several examples that the employees had used to explain their point. These helped me to understand, and I was able to work on letting loose of the reins and allowing others to assume more responsibility.

(Business owner)

True leaders welcome feedback. They understand that they need feedback from individuals, both inside and outside of the organization, to avoid losing touch with the everyday realities. While they understand that they cannot be what others want or think they should be, they value input from others as an important part of their journey of self-discovery.

If you are in a leadership position, I challenge you to create the conditions that will allow the people who report to you to do an honest evaluation of how you lead. After all, they have seen how you react to all types of situations, including those involving high levels of stress and pressure.

One way to get honest feedback from your employees is by using the services of a third party. This individual can be given direct access to your people. They can then report back to you in a way that will convey your employees' ideas without revealing anything specific enough to put any individual in jeopardy.

Training Programs and Evaluation Instruments

Numerous studies have been conducted over the years to identify what makes a leader. The results of these studies are used in leadership training programs. In most such programs, the participants evaluate their leadership qualities through a combination of instruments, self-reflection, and feedback from others. Information about such programs can be obtained from most reputable management consultants and from the continuing education department of the nearest university.

Feedback from One or More Key Individuals

Developing good relations with one or more key individuals can help you avoid the tendency to isolate yourself from hearing the bad news about the organization and about yourself. Even then, there may be some hesitancy on their part to be completely open until you prove that you are capable of accepting this type of information without recrimination.

Talking with individuals from outside the company can also provide valuable added information so long as these people know enough about you and your operation to make their feedback meaningful.

> The way I try to make sure that I'm keeping my head screwed on straight is by meeting regularly with my two closest associates within the company and by having quarterly meetings with three people outside of the company, whom I trust, and all of whom care enough about my continued success to ask me hard questions.
>
> It's probably not a perfect system, but it provides a lot of feedback that otherwise I wouldn't get.
>
> (CEO)

TRY TAKING YOURSELF A LITTLE LESS SERIOUSLY

Finally, try taking yourself a little less seriously. Be able to laugh at yourself now and then. One of the things that sometimes keeps a person in a leadership position from being able to ask for, or to accept, any form of feedback or criticism on his or her performance is some mistaken notion that to do so is a sign of weakness or vulnerability. In reality, the person who can ask for constructive criticism indicates that he or she possesses a high level of self-esteem and self-confidence and is interested in continuing to grow.

To help take yourself a little less seriously, you might think about how many times your orders are like those of the king on asteroid 325 in *The Little Prince* (New York: Light Year Press, Inc., 1992):

> The little prince plucked up his courage to ask the king a favor: 'I should like to see a sunset . . . Do me that kindness . . . Order the sun to set . . .'

The king responded, 'You shall have your sunset. I shall command it. But, according to my science of government, I shall wait until conditions are favorable.'

'When will that be?' inquired the little prince.

'Hum! Hum!' replied the king; and before saying anything else he consulted a bulky almanac. 'Hum! Hum! That will be about—about—that will be this evening about twenty minutes to eight. And you will see how well I am obeyed!'

Or you might think about the framed sign that the late Ray Wilkes had on his wall during the years he served as dean of the Ohio University branch campus at Lancaster, Ohio. The sign read:

I must hurry!

There they go,

And I Am Their Leader!

Taking Stock

The first step in ensuring that you continue to grow on the job is to develop a personal operating philosophy.

Next, it is important to create situations that will allow you to get meaningful feedback from others. None of us is capable of seeing ourselves exactly as others see us. Use as many approaches as you can to get feedback from others, and then make good use of the information you receive.

Chapter 11

Bringing Honor to the Profession of Business Leadership

In the liberated workplace, the leader assumes a new role that is more challenging, as well as more satisfying. The challenge lies in the leader's ability to exercise "invisible influence" while acting as the steadying influence in the workplace. The leader experiences satisfaction when people are liberated to do their best and to be their best. The leader in this liberation process, becomes a combination of servant, facilitator and guide.

CHARACTERISTICS OF THE LIBERATED WORKPLACE

Each Person Retains His or Her Own Unique Identity

In some relationships, whether they be personal or work related, one individual's personality becomes dominant. In work situations, the dominant person is usually the individual with authority or ruling power. We have already looked at many of the ways that some individuals misuse power and their employees' resulting loss of self-esteem and personal identity.

In the liberated workplace, the boss is still the boss, but no one is dominated for the sake of power or control. Individuals are appreciated for the gifts and talents they possess. Everyone is encouraged to share his or her abilities for the betterment of the whole.

What results is a team effort that features different individuals at different times, based upon the utilization of each person's gifts.

In this type of environment, the leader may at times act as the catalyst that rouses minds and spirits. At other times, the leader may serve as a team member or may seem invisible in the process. The leader assumes different roles to obtain the appropriate results.

When Working Together, Those Involved Develop a Mutual Identity

When individuals work together in this type of environment, each retains his or her individuality, but also becomes part of a team. The team thrives by combining the best from each individual into an approach that surpasses what any of the individuals could have accomplished alone. As the team forms, a new identity develops. This new identity does not clearly describe any one of the participants. Rather, it describes the team since it reflects the shared gifts of all its members. Ultimately, each team member has an individual identity and is part of the mutual identity which describes the team itself.

The leader is responsible for maintaining an atmosphere that encourages both individual and team growth and development. This is not an easy task, since the natural tendency is to deal with the strengths of individuals. However, the leader understands that ultimately, the best that results from shared gifts will surpass the best that can be produced by any individual. The key here is patience on the part of the leader, so that both the individuals and the team can develop and function their fullest potentials.

The Parameters of the Workplace Are Defined by Mutually Accepted Goals

As is the case in other work environments, goal setting is an integral part of the planning process in the liberated workplace. However, in this setting, employee involvement in the goal-setting process is based on mutual respect. The result is an open exchange of ideas and a sharing of information that will normally result in mutually accepted goals. Strategies to ensure accomplishment of these goals are then devised, and individual responsibilities are established.

Within the parameters of such a system, individuals operate freely, with an aura of confidence, and without the need to seek permission before acting since consent is implied by the manner in which the goals were developed. Success will depend upon open, two-way communication and a high level of mutual trust.

When this type of system is functioning smoothly, an outsider might question the need for a leader. The self-confident leader views this as a compliment, since success is reflected by the team's ability to take charge. This is "invisible influence" at its best.

Growth Is Continuous

In the liberated workplace, growth is occurring on a continuous basis in two areas: mental growth and spiritual growth.

Mental Growth. Because of the open and supportive environment, individuals look for growth opportunities. They learn from others on the job and take advantage of opportunities to increase their formal education.

Spiritual Growth. This is learning on a different plane. In the liberated work setting, individuals are open to seeing the good and emulating it. Or, at other times, they are comfortable doing what is right because it is right and having others emulate them.

The leader's primary responsibility in this area is to work to maintain a climate that promotes honesty, respect, and value-based decision making.

There Is a High Level of Tolerance for Divergent Methods and Opinions

More often than not, there is more than one right way to accomplish a task, or reach a goal. In the liberated workplace, individuals are encouraged to offer their best ideas and solutions, which can be combined with the suggestions of others.

Sometimes, time constraints will limit such discussions. However, within the constraints of each situation, tolerant consideration will be given to each individual's suggestions and ideas.

Throughout this process, the leader should encourage open discussion and full participation by all of the team members and discourage criticism of ideas, which could limit the amount of free exchange that will take place.

WITHOUT THE RIGHT TO DISAGREE, AGREEMENT IS MEANINGLESS

Regardless of the open nature of the liberated workplace, the leader is still in the position to have the final say on any issue. What is different is that, in this setting everyone else also has a say. Theirs may not be the final say, but liberation of the human spirit cannot exist unless each individual has the right to voice his or her opinion and openly disagree with the leader's position. Further, the liberation process demands that the leader assume that disagreements are offered in a spirit of shared responsibility by committed individuals who feel a deep sense of involvement in workplace outcomes.

NEEDED, A NEW STYLE OF LEADER

After 31 years with the company, it was my last day on the job. I was in my office waiting for my wife to arrive to accompany me to a little reception that the board had planned.

Stephen, one of my V.P.'s, came to the door and asked if he could see me for a minute.

I waved him in, and as he entered he shut the door.

"Before you leave, there is one other thing that I have to say. Thanks for being a friend, as well as a hell of a boss these past 10 years. I don't expect to ever tell another CEO that he is full of it or that one of his ideas is crazy."

I started to speak but Stephen held up his hand to stop me.

"I just wanted you to know that I am going to miss you more than you'll ever know."

At that point, I could see he had tears in his eyes.
We smiled at one another, and he left.
It was a moment that I have always cherished, and it means more with each passing year.

(Retired CEO)

Leading in the liberated workplace is leadership at its best. Those who are successful will possess many gifts in varying degrees. However, in order to be aware of a calling to *free others*, the liberating leader must have a reverence for the dreams and hopes of others and must be able to love others enough to delicately handle vulnerabilities that are exposed during the work relationship.

Words like *reverence* and *love* aren't found in every book on good business practices. However, we all have experienced their effects during our working careers. Sometimes, situations that involve reverence and love are described with words such as: *care, respect,* and *trust.* Even if we never use the "L" word at our workplace, its effects are going to be there if we trust others and do the things necessary to be trustworthy ourselves.

Leadership is about people and the ways that people work together to get things done. The person who is identified as a leader will earn that recognition by humanizing the workplace. Call it what you will, but that humanizing process requires reverence and love.

A PROFESSIONAL CALLING

To provide an environment in which individuals can do the following is as exciting as any career I can imagine:

* Maximize their potential while performing meaningful work that results in a needed product or service.

- Continue to grow as human beings.
- Be proud of and recognized for their accomplishments.
- Maintain their individuality, even while performing as a member of an effective team.
- Be happy.

At the same time, it is a career that has a profound effect on the lives of those who rely on the leader to create a freeing environment. It is, in my opinion, a professional calling that requires individuals of the highest order.

ATTAINING EXCELLENCE IN LEADERSHIP

I read a quotation once that captures the essence of the leader's job:

To Attain Excellence In Leadership:
   Care more than others think is wise.
   Risk more than others think is safe.
   Dream more than others think is practical.
   Expect more than others think is possible.

Care More Than Others Think Is Wise

Care is a word that many would not associate with the role of the person who is in charge of others. For some, caring would even be viewed as a soft or wimpy character flaw in a supervisor or manager.

However, the true leaders of today care about those who work for them. They view employees as partners rather than subordinates. As such, these leaders take it for granted that their employees' needs are no different than their own.

Paraphrasing Abraham Maslow, the noted theorist, all of us have needs that serve as motivators of behavior so long as they remain unsatisfied. Maslow classified these needs as physiological, safety, social, self-esteem, and self-fulfillment. Maslow also said that there is a hierarchy to our needs, in that our basic physiological needs must be satisfied in order for us to be motivated to satisfy our safety needs, and so forth.

Leaders care about the needs of others and utilize their positions to eliminate barriers that are beyond the capability of individuals to overcome on their own. Ultimately, the leader's goal is to create an environment in which others may live up to their potential or, in other words, live at their highest level of needs attainment.

> My father was rushed to the hospital over a weekend. He had an operation for an aneurysm in his stomach and was placed in the critical care unit. I went to work on Monday but I was a mess. I told my boss what had happened. As we talked, I told her that my father would probably be in critical care for about 10 days. I explained that visiting was limited to a 15-minute period every three hours and that there were only four visiting times per day. When I finished, she said, "You know you can have time off if you need it, but if you want to work, plan on running down to the hospital for the 11 A.M. and the 2 P.M. visiting times. That will help you to know how he is doing."
>
> For the next seven work days, I did visit my father twice per day. Since we are in a small town, the hospital wasn't too far away. I was gone about 40 minutes each time.
>
> When everything was over and my father was home, I thanked my boss again for allowing me to visit during work. "Well, if it had been my father, I would have gone to visit, so I figured you would want to," she said.
>
> I never forgot how she handled that situation, and I saw her do things like that for other employees too.
>
> (Secretary)

Others can tell whether you care about them. Most would tell you their opinion if you asked them. Of course, we don't often ask.

To be successful in working with others, you have to care about what they think, feel, and believe. You have to treat them with the same respect you believe you should be shown. So, if you believe in the old approaches, like using threats and intimidation to get results, you need to rethink your position. Leaders understand that success depends on the use of new and better methods, and they realize that caring is the chief building block upon which new business relationships must be built.

Risk More Than Others Think Is Safe

A leader must provide clear direction and must make clear-cut decisions when they are needed.

Sometimes, it would be safer to wait—to analyze more data, to hope that conditions will change, to find out which way the corporate winds are blowing—but a leader does not always follow the safest path.

Risk taking is inherent in the leader's job. It is one of the elements that differentiates between leaders and managers. Leaders are able to analize situations, come to conclusions, analyze and then act upon them. They must be able to anticipate consequences that could result from decisions, and they must have the strength of their convictions in order to stand by those decisions.

There are other job-related areas that require the leader to be a risk taker. For instance, self-disclosure to fellow employees often requires a high level of risk taking.

We were at a weekend retreat for top managers of the company. The main purpose of the get-together was to talk strategies about next year's sales and marketing campaign. We were in a breakout session, and our group of seven included Dennis, one of the company's executive V.P.'s.

As can happen, we got sidetracked, and Bob, a sales exec,

told a joke that contained ethnic slurs that were graphic and insulting. When he finished, there was some laughter, and then a pause. It seemed like everyone was waiting for Dennis's reaction.

After a moment, Mike, a marketing executive from our northwest region, who reported to Dennis, spoke up. "I really didn't appreciate that joke, Bob. I doubt if you would have told it under other circumstances."

Bob started to speak but was interrupted by Dennis. "Mike is right, Bob. I think it would be best if we avoided that type of thing in the future. This company has made a strong commitment to eliminating biases. Let's move on."

Later, Mike told me that when he spoke up, he had no idea what type of reaction he might get, but he felt he had to say something anyway.

(Sales executive)

Leadership involves risk taking. It is one of the characteristics that eliminates the fainthearted and the overcautious from stepping forward and assuming the role of leader.

Dream More Than Others Think Is Practical

In a recent interview in *Industry Week* magazine (May 2, 1994, p. 13), Jack Welch, CEO of General Electric, said:

A successful leader can shock an organization and lead its recovery. An unsuccessful leader will shock an organization and paralyze it. So organizations constantly need to be regenerated. There's a constant flow of ideas, excitement, and energy that has to be put into an organization. And it has to keep getting better. The bar has to keep going up. . . .

Well, once upon a time we'd budget in the boardroom down the hall, and we'd be presenting a budget with inventory turns of 5.13. The finance person or someone would say, 'Why can't we get 5.26?'—Decimal points are nonsense. *Dreams* are exciting, not decimal points. . . .

If you believe in boundaryless behavior, GE will never stop regenerating. If I get hit by a train tomorrow, somebody else would jump in. The genie's out of the bottle. It's open. People are out there. My job is to find great ideas, exaggerate them, and spread them like hell around the business with the speed of light. . . .

Loyalty means giving people an opportunity. Our job is to provide an atmosphere where they can reach their *dreams*, where they can feel that their growth is unlimited.

Leaders have a knack of being able to combine the right amount of practicality with a dreamer's mentality. This results in an ability to see what is and what should be, along with some of what could be.

Expect More Than Others Think Is Possible

Expectations, or the lack thereof, play a major role in all of our lives. For instance, everyone knows how Rodger Bannister's breaking of the four-minute mile barrier made it "possible" for other runners to begin to do so with some regularity.

Every person who has ever played sports has had more than one pep talk about why "our" team is better than "their" team, and any coach will tell you how winning builds confidence and affects attitudes and expectations about winning again.

Leaders have the ability to expect positive results in situations where others are ready to throw in the towel. To some extent, they expect to succeed because they have been successful in the past. Leaders don't give up because, at some time in the past, they have experienced the "thrill of victory" when it looked like they were headed for "the agony of defeat," and the deciding factor was their sheer determination to be successful.

We had been working 12-hour shifts, seven days a week, for six weeks. Everyone was walking around like zombies, and tempers were getting frayed. On a Friday night, our supervisor told us to plan on shutting down an hour early for a meeting in the lunchroom.

When we went into the lunchroom, our plant manager was there and so was the CEO from out of town. There was a huge banner across the front of the room that read, "One More Week." There were also pizzas, soft drinks, and homemade ice cream. The plant manager and the CEO both gave talks, thanking us for our efforts. They explained that we would be past the crisis in one more week and that our efforts had saved our contract with the company's biggest customer.

We all celebrated, and everyone came to work the next night with a lighter step and a renewed sense of commitment.

(Production worker)

There is a saying attributed to Henry Ford:

> If you think you can, or
> If you think you can't,
> either way, you're right!

A leader helps others to think positively about the many things that are within their capabilities and to reach beyond self-imposed boundaries toward new heights.

I JUST WATCH WHAT THEY DO

As I said in the Introduction, leaders do things that cause others to recognize them as leaders. Leadership is not a spectator sport. It requires a lot of hard work and love for people who have the same need for respect and recognition and dignity that all of us possess. I can think of no greater honor than to be told, "I believe you," "I trust you," "I know you have my best interests at heart."

REALIZING YOUR POTENTIAL

When you accept the challenge to lead, you make a commitment to realize your potential as a human being. You set forth on a quest that can lead to a meaningful and purposeful life.

James Michener in *The Fires of Spring* (New York: Random House, 1966), appropriately expresses how leaders view this exciting challenge:

> "For this is a journey that men make to find themselves. If they fail in this, it doesn't matter much what else they find. Money, position, fame, many loves, revenge are all of little consequence; and when the tickets are collected at the end of the ride, they are tossed in a bin marked failure. But if a man happens to find himself, if he knows what he can be depended upon to do, the limits of his courage, the position from which he will no longer retreat, the extent of his dedication, then he has found a mansion which he can inhabit with dignity all the days of his life."

To accept the challenge to lead means to strive to turn dreams about better ways of working together into reality, and to bring dignity to the workplace and to the worker. It also means that when realities fail to match dreams, the leader must try again, with renewed vigor, secure in the knowledge that life, without such a commitment to ideals, would hold no purpose.

You will discover no shortages if you accept a call to lead, but you would be hard-pressed to find any career situation that would be as rewarding. Good luck!

GENERAL INDEX

A

Abrasive executive, and
feedback discouragement,
118–19

Absence from workplace, and
feedback discouragement,
120

Achievement recognition, and
respect, 47

Agreement and right to disagree,
131

American Management
Association, 44

Appraisal-excempt exective, and
feedback discouragement,
119–20

Assumptions, and mutual trust,
52–54

AT&T, 100

Attitude, and mutual trust, 52

Autocratic management, 8–10

Autry, James, 97

B

Bardwick, Judith, 89

Batten, Joe, 59

Beliefs documentation, and
operating philosophy, 115–17

Bennis, Warren, 81

Bickham, John R., xiii

Blanchard, Ken, 34

Block, Peter, 34, 103

Braham, Barbara, xiii–iv

Branden, Nathaniel, 57–58

Buscaglia, Leo, 54

Business leadership as
professional calling, 132–33

C

Campbell, Walter J., xiii

Caring, degree of, and leadership,
133–35

Carnegie, Andrew, viii

About the Author

William Bickham is the assistant general manager of an electric utility. For more than 30 years, he has held various positions in both manufacturing and service organizations. An MBA graduate from Xavier University, Mr. Bickham is also an adjunct faculty member at Ohio University, where he teaches courses in business and total quality management.

Other books of interest to you from Irwin Professional Publishing . . .

Rewarding and Recognizing Employees
Ideas for Individuals, Teams, and Managers
Joan P. Klubnik

Shows organizations how to initiate and maintain a dynamic reward/recognition program that will go a long way toward making employees feel genuinely valued and appreciated. (150 pages)

0-7863-0297-6

Inspiring Commitment
How to Win Employee Loyalty in Chaotic Times
Anthony Mendes

Shows how companies can use effective goal maintenance, decision making, and team building to gain the trust, loyalty, and commitment of the work force. Designed to motivate everyone from the CEO to the frontline worker. (125 pages)

0-7863-0422-7